MAKE YOUR MOVE

Alan Beaubien

Compliments of

MAKE YOUR MOVE:

*Change the way you look at your world
and change your bottom line*

ALAN BEAULIEU AND BRIAN BEAULIEU

With

Mark Steisel

New York

Make Your Move

Change the way you look at your world and change your bottom line

Cover Design by: 3 Dog Design   www.3dogdesign.net

Softcover ISBN: 978-1-60037-719-8

Hardcover ISBN: 978-1-60037-720-4

Library of Congress Control Number: 2009937701

MORGAN · JAMES
THE ENTREPRENEURIAL PUBLISHER

Morgan James Publishing
1225 Franklin Ave., STE 325
Garden City, NY 11530-1693
Toll Free 800-485-4943
www.MorganJamesPublishing.com

In an effort to support local communities, raise awareness and funds, Morgan James Publishing donates one percent of all book sales for the life of each book to Habitat for Humanity. Get involved today, visit www.HelpHabitatForHumanity.org.

Dedication

To our mother, Jeannine Beaulieu, who was a builder of dreams and never tired in having faith in us and encouraging us.

ACKNOWLEDGEMENTS

We wish to express our gratitude to many people who have impacted our lives in direct, meaningful and lasting ways.

First we need to thank our Dad, Norman Beaulieu, for instilling in us the value of hard work and the importance of business. Dad, thanks! Our wives, Dawn (Alan) and Joan (Brian) deserve all the gratitude we can muster. They have been very supportive and understanding in this endeavor and in our travel-laden careers. Dawn, thanks for the proof-reading and editing. Our children have given up a lot of 'Dad time" over the years and we thank them as well: Jackie, Ben, Jesslyn (Brian's) and Stephanie, Kimberly, Joseph, Nicole, Daniel and Michelle (Alan's).

We are privileged to work with wonderful people at ITR®. It takes many people to make a successful consulting firm work. We especially want to thank Debbie Brown for all the extra time and effort in helping us through this project. Joanne Houston, you have been there longer than we have and we thank you for all that you bring to ITR˚ and therefore how much you have contributed to this book. Andrew Duguay, thanks for the assist with the research.

Our good friend Jaynie Smith pushed us into actually doing this – thanks Jaynie! Vistage has played a key role in our lives and many people have given us great advice over the years. We wish to single out Rick Oppenheimer, States Hines, Allen Hauge and Richard Carr for their influence.

This is also the right time to express our gratitude and respect to two very important people: the originator of the cyclical theories we still use today – Chapin Hoskins and Helen Langwasser, his successor at the Institute for Trend Research. We are continuing that body of work today and inherent in that work is the study and application of the business cycle.

Last on the page, but only so that it will be remembered, is our gratefulness to God for the gifts, opportunities and life He has granted us. We are humbled and ever so grateful to be able to do this. We are also grateful for having been born twins. We cannot imagine any other kind of life and we would not want it any other way. Twins and best buds – does it get any better than that?

Table of Contents

INTRODUCTION

What would you do if you could predict the future? How would you position your business if you knew that a year from now your products would fly off the shelf or you couldn't give them away? If you could tell when changes would occur and what economic conditions would exist, you couldn't lose. You could make adjustments that would enable you to prosper in upturns, downturns, and recessions —even in depressions.

Make Your Move: Change the way you look at your world and change your bottom line will teach you how to forecast future economic developments and explain how you should prepare for them. This action-oriented book will clearly tell you how to:

- Understand the importance of business cycles - what they are and how they work

- Pinpoint what phase of the business cycle your business is in

- Understand leading indicators and those that apply to your business

- Spot changes in the business cycle well before they take place

- Take specific steps to capitalize on those changes and boost your company's bottom line.

For the past 27 years, through our tenure with the Institute for Trend Research, we have specialized in forecasting future economic changes. In that time, we have compiled a 96% accuracy record that has helped our clients to increase their profits and build for the future — even in the most severe economic downturns. In order to make our forecasts, we study scores of economic factors and isolate those that show the changes which will occur. We call these isolated factors leading indicators. Then we compile statistical information from a number of leading indicators, examine them, and determine whether they relate to particular businesses and industries. Finally, we estimate when changes will occur and advise our clients what to do.

As the term implies, leading indicators give us information about forthcoming changes before those changes occur. Each leading indicator has its own lead-time, which is an estimate of how long it will take for the change evident in the indicator to take place in orders, sales, production, etc. When businesses follow our guidelines, they can predict changes 12 months in advance. This gives them plenty of time to be proactive to the business climate ahead.

> *Make Your Move* is a practical, action-oriented book, packed with solutions to problems that hundreds of thousands of businesses regularly face. In clear, nontechnical language, it explains precisely what steps to take and when to take them. Many of the solutions we recommend are counterintuitive; so, without this book, you might be hard pressed to learn about them on your own. As a result, you could miss golden opportunities and could jeopardize your future.

For example, during Phase A of the business cycle, the economy is improving so businesses must become aggressive, make firm plans, and commit to expenditures to capitalize on the upcoming boom. However, most will not. They, like most of those around them, will be stuck in recession mindsets: hoarding money, employing skeletal staffs, and keeping inventories too low. They will be afraid to change and will just sit tight, which will decrease their future profits and affect their very survival.

Our approach

Although economics affects all of us, few understand or know much about it. When the subject comes up, most people's eyes glaze over, and their minds turn off. Their reactions reflect the fact that economics has been presented in terms of mathematical equations (econometrics) and in ways that few comprehend. So most people consider the subject dense, beyond their grasp. As a result, they don't bother to listen or try to understand.

We've demystified economics by making it clearer and easier to understand. In fact, we've been told that we make it enjoyable and entertaining. Our approach is to simplify it, discuss it in clear terms and put it in a context that everyone can easily understand and retain. Plus, we try to inject a big dose of fun.

Our approach is to look at the economy as if it were a symphony because both are complex and interactive; both are built on intricate, intertwined layers. Both a symphony and the economy involve numerous players executing different notes, on different instruments, at different times. Yet, they all come together and produce amazing results. Usually, those results are harmonious, uplifting and even exhilarating, but they can also be dissonant, atonal, and out of synch.

A symphony and the economy have orchestral components that take place beyond the range of our hearing, which nonetheless are part of the whole. Although symphony halls are acoustically engineered, wild cards (ambient noise, audiences, and the unexpected) always intrude and alter the sounds each time a symphony is performed. Even when the perfect venue has been designed for the best per-

"ITR has always hit the mark," according to Robert Yung, CEO of Trico, a 90-year-old lubrication management services company. "The impact of ITR on our company is in the six figure range or multiples of that. The benefit of being prepared is huge and while it's hard to quantify, it's significant.'

formers, many factors can affect the listening experience. If those factors can be anticipated, the experience can be enhanced.

We look at the economy musically, not just mathematically or intellectually. The musician's soul feels how the disparate notes of the economy flow, fit together, change through time and have the purpose and direction to tell stirring tales. Too often, economic messages get lost in the details, in the explanations. So we encourage readers to lower their guards, open their minds, and approach the economy as if they were listening to great music — to sit back, relax and take it all in. As they listen to the whole, it will make sense. Occasionally, they can examine particular elements and reflect on their brilliance, but then they must come back to the unified whole and let its magic work.

The book

Make Your Move has been written in a clear, practical, and direct style with a straightforward, no-nonsense approach. It speaks directly to business people, gets right to the point, and recommends precise step-by-step, well-tested solutions that have been proven to work. The book is not theoretical. It does not include jargon, unnecessary repetition, or useless information. Instead, it is written to immediately grab the attention of busy, intelligent people who have little spare time. If we must say so ourselves, it is a lively, enjoyable, eye opening read to which you will constantly refer; and we hope — recommend.

To make it easy to understand and retain, *Make Your Move* is filled with practical recommendations, anecdotes, examples, checklists, and charts. All information has been broken into easily digestible chunks. The result is a comprehensive, information-packed book that will give you concrete help that you can immediately apply.

Now is the time

We are coming through very tough times. The stock market tanked and then recovered some of the lost ground; yet joblessness is setting new highs. The economy is reeling and businesses everywhere are at a loss to know if a double-dip downturn awaits us. Others wonder if this will be a V shaped recovery or a prolonged slump. Their leaders don't know what to do, where to turn, or what the future holds. You can know what is coming and you can know how it will impact your business.

Now is the time to make your move! Begin by reading this book. *Make Your Move* is a book for these unprecedented times. Although the economy is now depressed, it will improve. So you need to know when the recovery will start in earnest for your business. By the time you finish reading this book you will be prepared to make the most of the upswing when it takes hold for you. This book will help you and other business leaders escape your recession mentalities and take decisive actions to position your companies for better days. *Make Your Move* will act as your guide and provide the blueprint for your future success.

Chapter 1
How Business Cycles Drive Profits

The use of history is to give value to the present hour and its duty.
Ralph Waldo Emerson

I magine if you could predict the future. What would you have done differently in 1999 if you knew with a high degree of certainty that there would be a recession in 2000? How about if you had known in 2007 and early 2008 that the devastating global financial crisis would paralyze us in 2009?

The fact is you can know, you can tell what economic changes lay ahead, because they are signaled well in advance. And these signals give all of us plenty of time to adjust to what is coming next.

David J. Morse and Jonathan Hsu head 24/7 Real Media, a digital marketing company that started using our economic forecasts in its strategic and operational planning in 2004. At that time, the US and global economies were strong and our analysis confirmed that it would remain that way through 2007. Our advice to David and

Jonathan was straightforward; be aggressive, hire more people and expand the business. They took our advice and used their skills and expertise to expand their business. In the next few years, 24/7 grew into a $250 million company that employed 400 people worldwide.

In 2006, we saw that the business cycle would decline in 2008 and 2009. So we told David and Jonathan that it would be tough to be a stand-alone company in 2008 and that they should consider selling the business because at that time, buyers were paying top dollar. They decided to follow our advice, and in 2007, they sold their company for $649 million, which was the optimum return for them, their employees and shareholders.

24/7 was able to capitalize on our advice in another way. It shifted its focus from Western Europe to Canada and Australia, where it has been very successful at capturing market share while reaping record profits. At the same time, the company also stepped up its employee training so it could provide top-notch service. As a result, it is now the top interactive network in Canada and they are climbing steadily in Australia.

Their success as leaders is impressive and measurable. 24/7 has thrived over the last few years while its competitors have seen their revenues and profits dip sharply. Can you use the business cycle to your advantage? You bet you can!

Showing businesses where to look for clues to the future and what that future will be is our job — no, it's more than that, it is our mission and our passion. Business cycles are real and we believe that helping you prepare for these inevitable changes will not only protect your profits, but will make life better for you, your families, your employees and their families. Oh, and one more thing – we are convinced that by working with you to make your company stronger, we also help make the country healthier, stronger and more globally competitive.

Suppose you knew that a year from now that your products would be in great demand or conversely, that no one would be buying them?

How would you position your business?

- Could you strengthen your business by decreasing your costs, raising your prices or stocking up on the goods you will need?

- How many potential problems could you avoid?

- What would you need in terms of people and capital in order to meet the coming challenges (both good and bad, up and down)?

- Should you look to expand?

These questions are not abstract because, believe it or not, you can consistently forecast what the upcoming business climate will be and turn it to your advantage. You can predict a year in advance whether the demand for your goods or services will increase or if your cost of doing business will soar. Armed with that information, you can make decisions to boost your profits, strengthen your company and avoid the same traps that are driving your competitors out of business. It all revolves around business cycles. Here's how it works.

Cycles

Cycles are a part of life and nature; they are inherent in every aspect of our world. We and virtually everything around us— all living things — go through cycles. Our bodies pass through phases: periods of ups, downs, growth, stagnation and change. Each day moves from morning to afternoon and night; light turns to darkness. The seasons — winter, spring, summer and fall — come in cycles, as do waves, winds, storms and other natural events. Quantum physics and harmonics even suggest that all matter moves in regular patterns. Cycles are a normal part of life. We all accept, expect, and plan for them.

Since cycles are so pervasive, it stands to reason that they would also exist in our economy. Those economic cycles are called business cycles and they have existed since at least the 1400s (as shown by the cyclical studies of Chapin Hoskins). Chart 1-1 shows the tip of the iceberg — the business cycles that have occurred since 1900.

20th Century Business Cycles

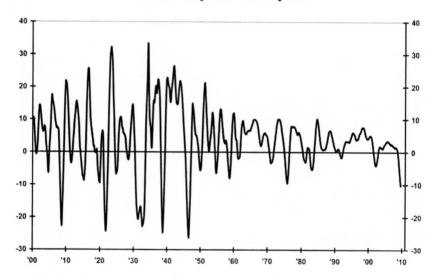

CHART 1-1. BUSINESS CYCLES SINCE 1900 TO 2009.
Chart of the 12/12 rate-of-change for US Industrial Production 1900 through mid 2009.

Business cycles are measured from their low points, from trough to trough. Here's how they work:

- The *upside* is the positive slope and is measured from trough to peak, low to high. It is a fertile period in which most companies grow and thrive. Being ready for these good times is essential if you want to maximize your growth and profits.

- The *backside* is the negative slope and is measured from peak to trough, high to low. Although the backside of the business cycle tends to bring tougher times for most businesses, it can usher in incredible opportunities for those who are both aware and prepared.

Company Sales to US Industrial Production
12/12 Rates-of-Change

CHART 1-2. This chart shows how a company's sales (the broken line) vacillate up and down in concert with the overall business cycle (the bold line). Our objective at the Institute for Trend Research is to make sure our client companies *outperform* the general business cycle.

Most business leaders understand that business cycles exist. However, we can all get so immersed in the day-to-day details of running our businesses that we don't stop to think about how the cycles will impact us. We don't ask where we are in the business cycle and we don't consider the actions that we can take to capitalize on the changes that will come. The irony is that by the time so many business leaders figure out something is wrong, it's often too late to avoid the problem or effectively be proactive about it.

It's not hard to convince business people that business cycles exist, but it's very difficult to get them to do anything about them including anticipating when they might occur and what plans they should make. Don't fall into this trap! We tell our clients that "you can't change the wind, but you can adjust the sails."

Like sailors, business leaders must know which way the winds are blowing in order to get their companies from Point A to Point B most effectively.

Universality

Businesses don't operate in vacuums and are not immune to events outside their particular spheres. Today's world is smaller, and virtually all companies work within larger environments that affect whether they grow, prosper, and even survive. As we write, businesses that had nothing to do with housing have fallen victim to the housing-induced recession because housing is such a large, far-reaching part of our economy. Although all of us didn't buy mortgage-backed securities or get involved with credit default swaps, we all have been victimized by that great credit debacle.

Similarly, the impact of domestic business cycles is not limited to the US. The impact of cycles leapfrogs traditional borders and affects business in other countries, especially our major trading partners: Canada, the UK, Germany, Japan, India, and China. Conversely, when business cycles occur abroad, we feel them in the US.

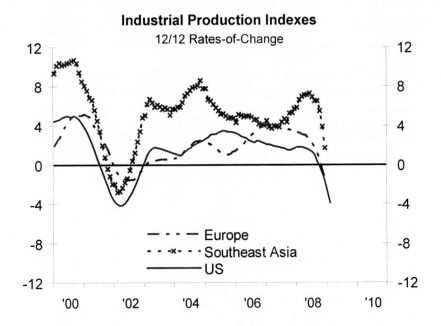

CHART 1-3. The world tends to go through similar cycles at the same time. Globalization and financial networks have increased this fact. Rises and declines in a geographic area of importance, such as Europe and/or the US, will have consequences throughout the rest of the global economy.

Our work has shown us that business cycles affect all types of businesses, regardless of their size, but start-ups are more prone to being business-cycle proof. Since start-ups are just getting off the ground, they're usually focused on one of two objectives: (1) taking market share from someone else or (2) serving 100% of an expanding market that they probably created — which is the essence of beating the business cycle. Beating the business cycle comes naturally to start-ups; it's inherent in what they do. It is instinctively what entrepreneurs do, how they think, how they look at the world.

Most start-ups also have the advantage of having a clean slate, low overhead, streamlined decision-making processes, and the ability to make changes on the fly. Incoming cash is usually funneled right back into the business with an eye to doing even more business expansion/ innovation tomorrow. Long hours and an aggressive energy are the norm. So going into business during a downturn may not be a bad idea because you're able to act quickly and race ahead of older, slower-to-react companies, particularly if you know how long the bad times will last and how much working capital you will need.

The impact

Cycles are important because the economy goes through ups that are favorable for growing business and downs in which business disappears. If business operators understand where they are in the business cycle, they can make the most of the conditions that lie ahead. How well they prepare depends on knowing where they are in a cycle, the type of cycle involved, and reading the road signs to the future. Those road signs are the leading indicators that we will introduce to you in the next chapter.

We have identified four phases within each business cycle: Phases A, B, C and D. Since each phase of the cycle has its own strengths and traps, businesses must use management tactics that are specific to each phase to ensure their prosperity. The four business cycle phases are:

> *Phase A — Advancing.* The economy is on the upswing; advancing toward better days.
> *Phase B — Best.* Business conditions are booming.
> *Phase C — Caution.* The economy is still growing, but at a slower pace. Phase C is the most profitable phase of the business cycle, but it is also time to become more conservative in your planning.
> *Phase D — Danger.* The downward stage. People are depressed. It is time to keep the powder dry and be ready for action!

Knowing what phase of the business cycle you're in and the actions you should take will impact your profitability today and how your company is positioned for the long haul.

MAKE YOUR MOVE >>> We all can adjust to economic ups and downs, and indeed highly successful companies regularly do so. During the favorable phases of the business cycle, be sure to have *enough*: enough of the right people, enough training, enough inventory; plus sufficient capital, machinery, and equipment to meet the increased demand. When the business climate is favorable, it may be a great time to increase prices.

When the business cycle is just beginning to turn up, companies that are not convinced that the demand for their items will rise usually are reluctant to increase the factors of production needed to make the most of the rising trend. And, when increased demand comes, they won't be able to satisfy it or they will have to run out and buy what they need at a time when it will cost more for overtime, rushed shipments, air deliveries, raw material bottlenecks, etc. If you can't see the coming rising trend, you won't be in position to fully capitalize on this golden opportunity — in fact, you may even lose out to more far-seeing competitors.

When the business cycle is down, it becomes even harder for business because everyone hopes the downturn will be brief. Many organizations suffer by not acting quickly enough in:

- Laying off employees.
- Shifting to strong cash positions.
- Decreasing inventory levels.
- Watching their receivables, credit, and debt.
- Looking hard to be sure return on investment will justify all capital expenditures.

> ### *In a business cycle trough, cash and preparation rule the roost.*

Business leaders who don't pay attention to business cycles are likely to be swept along with the herd. They'll lose control of their direction, be forced to move with the pack and could be consumed in the frenzied stampede. Many will be trampled. As they're left broken and bleeding, they still won't have a clue as to what happened. They'll claim that no one could have foreseen it; that their downfall came completely out of the blue — which simply isn't true. Since business cycles are telegraphed at least a year in advance, they should have paid attention and should have known what changes were at hand.

ALAN SAYS

I remember talking to a group of CEO's on the West Coast in 2000, a recession year. I showed them a graph that demonstrated the cyclical nature of the US economy and the direct cyclical relationship between the macroeconomic cycles and what businesses are willing to spend on IT, specifically on equipment and software. In good times, businesses spend more money on IT. When the economy falls into recession, a clear and related contraction takes place.

After my presentation, a young entrepreneurially-minded software executive/engineer approached me. He was obviously a bright fellow with a strong desire to succeed. He said that his industry was not impacted by economic forces and added that no one could see a change (like a recession) coming. I wondered if his company was an exception to the rule or perhaps a start-up. I asked how his business was doing on a year-over-year basis. The answer — *down*! Furthermore, the office building he owned was experiencing increased vacancies.

What did I learn? Simply this: the entrepreneurial spirit is so alive and strong in some of us that we don't *believe* that the business cycle exists or that the economy will impact us. Instead, we are certain that we are the sole masters of our fates. This belief often persists despite external and internal evidence to the contrary.

Variations

Business cycles differ. Throughout history, the economy has gone through industrial cycles, monetary cycles, and price cycles. The patterns of the various cycles vary in their durations and in their ebbs and flows. Our current analysis shows that we're passing through a price-cycle trough and that we will have many years of inflationary pressures ahead.

Cycles, regardless of their kind and intensity, ultimately change. These changes may take time, but they always occur. For example, we can't stay bogged in periods of deflation forever because people would end up giving goods away. We also can't endure endless inflation because eventually no one could afford to buy anything. So the economy will always

Have you ever noticed that when the economy has been strong for a couple of years, how many pundits and business articles pronounce the business cycle dead? Throughout history, business cycles have existed, and they will continue to influence our economy because the same underlying essentials that caused previous cycles still exist. These essentials are all related to supply and demand, consumerism, and the desire to improve one's standing in life and accumulate wealth. Certain forces don't change, including human nature. Those who reject the existence of business cycles have consistently been proven wrong when cycles occur, such as the 2008-2009 downturn.

Although governments feel that it's their role to minimize swings in the economic cycle, government intervention rarely works. Going a step further, history has shown us that when totalitarian governments try to interrupt economic cycles through massive intervention, the result has been human suffering, people have no drive, many starve and others simply move into survival mode. Government intervention, however well intentioned, can be extremely dangerous!

adjust according to the opportunities that occur. This continuous adjustment process is part of the beauty and wonder of capitalism.

The industrial business cycle is a wave that runs for about 52 years and it impacts most businesses. Within this long wave, four 13-year cycles exist (they are similar to the four 13-week quarters found within a 52-week year). If you look into a 13-year cycle, you will find there are three or four smaller business cycles that are three to four years in duration when measured from trough to trough. Plan for the changes that occur in these three to four year business cycles because they can have a powerful impact on your company's profitability and even its viability over the long term.

Remember

In business, competition is fierce. As soon as a product or service hits the market, someone, somewhere can make it faster, cheaper or just as well and deliver it anywhere in no time flat. So companies have to be efficient and maximize their profits.

Understanding the business cycle, knowing where the economy is in the business cycle and when conditions are likely to change will give you a competitive edge. It will enable you to enhance your company's profits through the timely implementation of well-thought-out and sharply-focused plans.

Knowing where your company fits in the business cycle will also boost your personal success. If you know where your company stands and how the climate is changing, you can assess your alternatives and make the best decisions. In the following chapters, we will help you make those decisions. We will discuss, in detail, the specific Management Objectives™ that are appropriate in each phase of the business cycle because each phase has its own unique psychology and challenges, which can provide outstanding opportunities for forward-thinking executives.

Chapter 2
Trend Indicators

History is but the unrolled scroll of prophecy.

James A. Garfield

Getting a handle on the economy is not as difficult as you might think. It comes down to following proven, reliable signals that reveal how the economy is going to perform in the future. These signals are called leading indicators.

In our forecasts, we use a number of leading indicators, which we will describe below. Each leading indicator has a lead-time that helps us determine when the actual change will occur. For example, changes in corporate bond prices indicate how US Industrial Production will perform in 10 to 12 months.

Unfortunately, all too frequently, business leaders don't spring into action when they see the leading indicators change. In fact, they often become paralyzed, fearful, and don't know when to act. Usually, they worry that the indicators may be faulty and steer them wrong, so they're afraid to take the risk. Plus, it's comfortable sitting tight, not adjusting for the coming cycle until others do. It's the old "safety in numbers" game, hiding in the middle of the pack — where you're likely to get boxed in.

> ***MAKE YOUR MOVE>>>*** To avoid being trapped, take a *systemic* approach; that way you can protect yourself if any one or two of the indicators are out of synch and provide false signals. False signals can appear when certain indicators reflect activity unique to a particular sector and not to others. So protect yourself by using leading indicators to forecast economic change in the following way:

What to do

- *Set up a system of leading indicators.* Find the indicators that apply to your business and use them to forecast future changes. Include those that we describe below and add any others that you have used or that might help.

- *When two of your leading indicators go up or down, pay attention.* Take notice and look to see whether other leading indicators confirm that a change in direction is real. At the Institute, we calculate the probabilities that trends will reverse using shortcuts that we will discuss later in this book. When two of your leading indicators tell you that the wind has begun to shift, start planning because planning takes time. Decide which sails must be set and who will be manning the ropes.

- *When five leading indicators reverse direction, act.* It's usually solid evidence that the economy is turning. Move forward with confidence because the system is telling you that a fundamental shift in the momentum of the economy is taking place. When five leading indicators move in the same way, it's rarely a coincidence. Each indicator that signals a reversal confirms the other indicators and verifies that the economy will shift in a new direction. When five leading indicators agree, have your resources lined up and be ready to implement your plan because change is on the way. Many people will feel their adrenaline pumping because economic conditions are about to get exciting again!

- *Start making the tactical changes needed to implement your strategic plan.* If it turns out that the shift in the leading indicators is misleading or incomplete, you will not have overreacted. You will have simply flexed the corporate muscles you will need when the change in the business cycle has been either internally or externally verified.

Since all businesses differ, you may be wondering if tracking leading indicators will work for you. In the vast majority of cases, the answer is "yes". We know this because we've tested it. According to the data we have received from a wide variety of businesses, almost all companies can rely on leading indicators to accurately forecast future changes. The leading indicators discussed below and other concepts that we will tell you about later in this book will let you learn what the future holds in store for your business.

BRIAN SAYS

John, a savvy VP of marketing and sales guy in the industrial and agriculture markets, looked at the economy as if it were a train. He knew his company wasn't the engine or the caboose so he constantly paid close attention to which cars would go through the valley before him. By always watching the other cars, John learned when new sales opportunities would start to present themselves so that he could plan and be more aggressive with his pricing. By the way, watching the other cars also helped John sell his business when the business cycle was at its peak.

John sold the business as the business cycle reached its high. He was able to sell for top dollar because he never stopped watching the railroad cars in front of him.

Strong indicators

In making our forecasts, we use a number of the leading indicators. Here are some of the major indicators we use:

1. Corporate bond prices:

12/12 Rate-of-Change: Tracking the movement in corporate bond prices is an outstanding leading indicator that many forecasters overlook. We've been using it for a long time and find it extremely valuable.

If you've heard us speak, you know that tracking corporate bond prices is one of our favorite

---

WARNING:

Don't act when just one leading indicator changes. When two leading indicators turn, watch for developing signs in those particular series and keep scanning other leading indicators. Act when five leading indicators, each confirming the others, move in the same direction. You need five leading indicators to change before you can verify that a new broad-based economic trend is about to occur.

---

leading indicators. We love its accuracy and prize its objectivity. The Corporate Bond Prices 12/12 rate-of-change has worked extremely well no matter which political party was in control of the White House or Congress. It's been accurate in times of war or peace, inflation, deflation, changes in the Federal Reserve Board leadership and the increased globalization of the past 20 years. Even the introduction of disco in the 1970s didn't disrupt the value of the Corporate Bond Prices 12/12 as a leading indicator!

How it works: If the prices for bonds that are being sold through the exchanges are rising, it means that bond yields are going down, which is good for corporations because their cost of borrowing money will be less. That shows that corporate leadership is not afraid of inflation and the lower interest rates make it easier to invest in new capital equipment and new enterprises.

- High interest rates discourage borrowing money.
- Low interest rates encourage the use of credit.

So we want to see rising corporate bond prices because it means that more businesses can borrow money and use it to build their businesses and revenues. Corporate bond prices are one of the earliest leading indicators. Although changing corporate bond prices are the first sign of a trend the vast majority of the time, few people know that they should track them.

Lead-time: Changes in corporate bond prices indicate that adjustments in the overall economy will usually occur in approximately 10 months. We advise clients that they have four quarters lead-time.

Sources: Information on corporate bond prices can be obtained from Moody's Investor Services (www.moodys.com), Bloomberg (www. bloomberg.com) and other financial services. Every month, look at the average yield for Double-A rated or Triple-A rated corporate bonds.

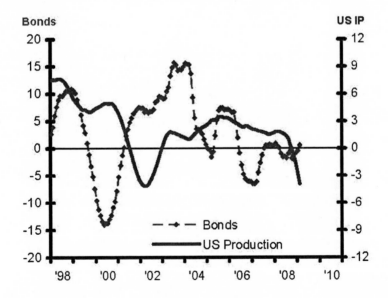

CHART 2-1. This chart shows how leading indicators fit within the framework of the overall economy is not always intuitive. Note the big drop in bond prices in 2000 and how it led the 2002 drop in industrial production.

2. EcoTrends® Leading Indicator: This important indicator was developed by Brian in the late 1980s and has been modified periodically since. It's a composite index that we've put together to strike a balance between two parts of our economy: consumer and industrial behavior.

How it works: The EcoTrends® Leading Indicator shows whether business-to-business activity and business-to-consumer activity are going up or going down. It contains items such as financial indicators (stock market, bond market or money supply), a widely accepted consumer measure (housing starts or retail sales) and new orders for goods. If you try to construct your own index, make sure to balance all of the leading indicators.

Lead-time: Highs range from 12 to 19 months ahead with the median being 17 months. The median lead-time for lows is 15 months.

Sources: Consumer and new order information can be found through government agencies such as the Department of Commerce, Department of Labor and the Federal Reserve Board. Data on the financial indicators are published in the Wall Street Journal and other publications and websites.

3. Institute for Supply Management (ISM) Purchasing Managers Index: This is a top-notch leading indicator. It takes a different slant from tracking corporate bond prices, which looks at corporate finances, and the EcoTrends® Leading Indicator, which examines a mixture of business activities. The Purchasing Managers Index is based on a compilation of statistics based on surveys of purchasing managers. The ISM Purchasing Managers Index is best suited for following the business-to-business side of our economy.

How it works: This Index provides a good composite from the order side of business. It gathers information from purchasing managers and examines whether inventories, prices, order activity, exports, and imports are going up or down, and if delivery times are accelerating or slowing.

ISM has done an excellent job of weighting this index so it consistently leads the economy through highs and lows. It provides a good indication of the overall temperature of the business community.

Lead-time: The typical lead-time is about seven months through lows and five months through highs before a similar change will be seen in the economy as measured by US Industrial Production.

Sources: This information can be found on the front page of any newspaper business section or at the ISM website www.ism.ws.

4. US Leading Indicator*: Originally compiled by the government, this is now put together and issued by The Conference Board, a private concern. It's a good indicator that is heavily weighted toward the consumer side of the economy.

How it works: Among other items, the US Leading Indicator tracks the number of building permits issued. It has been negative in 2008 and early 2009 and it won't improve until the housing market starts coming back. Other components are money supply, stock market, spread in interest rates, building permits, manufacturers' new orders for nondefense capital goods, manufacturers' new orders for consumer goods and materials, average weekly manufacturing hours, index of consumer expectations, index of supplier deliveries (vendor performance), and state initial claims for unemployment insurance.

Lead-time: The typical lead time at highs is 13 months and 10 months at lows.

Source: The Conference Board issues the US Leading Indicator via press releases. It is also reported in newspapers and can be accessed at www. conference-board.org.

5. Orders vs. Inventory Levels: This tracks both the number of orders for products and the level of company inventories.

How it works: When orders are increasing and inventories are declining, it's a good indication that the economy is growing stronger. If orders are going down and inventories are growing, it indicates that we are getting into a recession. We have a ratio that we use to calculate this information called RIO, which stands for ratio of inventory to orders.

Lead-time: 11 months through highs and 7 months on the median.

Source: The figures on new orders and inventories are distributed by the US Department of Commerce in its M3 Release. Interested parties can contact the Department to access this release.

6. Stock Market (S&P 500). The stock market is not one of our favorite forecasting indicators, but we look at it because so many others like it. We also like to try to figure out where the stock market is heading.

How it works: When stocks rise, most consider the economy to be moving in a positive direction, and the opposite holds true when the stock market declines. The problem with the stock market as a forecasting indicator is twofold: (1) movement in the market can be coincidental and (2) at times, the market has lagged behind the bulk of the economy. We've seen times when the stock market didn't peak until after a recession began.

On the other hand, the stock market generally reflects how well corporations are perceived to be doing. It also tracks a broad cross-section of the economy and is extremely popular, so we give it consideration.

Lead-time: Four months.

WARNING: Many people rely on various stock market indexes to gauge the future economic climate, and others rely on it exclusively.

However, these indexes don't give the full economic picture and are not terribly reliable leading indicators.

The stock market can be useful as a part of the total picture, but it is not reliable enough to stand on its own. To compound the problem, many people constantly check the Dow Jones, S&P and other indexes. They check them every day and frequently during each day, which can give them a false indication and confusing statistical noise that does not forecast real trends.

Sources: All major city and financial newspapers and online financial sites.

7. Housing starts: The change in the number of housing starts is a solid indicator that can be easily tracked. Since housing is such a huge part of the economy, the number of housing starts must be included in any leading indicator system for that system's projections to be accurate.

How it works: The number of houses started is collected and the larger the number the more beneficial impact it has on the economy. As we've mentioned, even though a business has nothing to do with housing, the number of housing starts can affect it because it ripples through the rest of the economy. Until the housing market starts showing some improvement, it's hard to say that recovery is at hand. Until housing starts pick up, the economy will continue to go through a lot of pain.

Lead-time: During highs, housing will lead industrial production by a median of eight months. For lows, the median is six months.

Sources: The US Census Bureau is a readily available source for information on housing starts. The statistics for housing starts are available by region so people can focus on the situation in their particular area. In some states, they are also available by counties.

8. Retail sales: The rate-of-change in retail sales is an extremely important indicator although it doesn't provide much actual lead time regarding changes in the bulk of the economy. During good times, retail sales account for 67% of the US economy.

How it works: When retail sales are down, the economy will not improve until consumers get back in the game. In trying to forecast change, retail sales is the last piece of the pie that must fall into place for you to know that a trend is real. When retail sales activity increases, you can feel very confident about the recovery and know that a new trend will soon take place.

Lead time: Retail sales have a relatively short lead time through both highs and lows of two and three months, respectively, to US Industrial Production.

Sources: US Government Census Bureau.

ECO-SENSE

Since you will be working with leading indicators, familiarize yourself with them. Go to the sources that we've cited in this chapter and review them. See what information they provide and how it's presented. Learn more about these sources because when you subsequently decide to use them, you will easily find what you need, which will save you lots of time.

Confirming indicators

Certain signals are not strong enough to indicate future change by themselves, but they are useful in confirming that a change is at hand. After five leading indicators show us that a new general economic trend is taking shape, we also look to the following items to further verify our findings. The confirming indicators we use include:

1. Change in temporary work force

Some forecasters look at how many temporary workers are being placed by agencies such as Manpower Inc. They believe that if these agencies are not placing a great many temps, it indicates that businesses are not confident about tomorrow or simply don't have as great a need for workers.

We use temporary worker placement as a confirming signal because the number of temporary placements made does not provide a strong glimpse into the future — especially when other indicators give us up to a 12-month advanced warning. However, the numbers of temps being placed should not be ignored because it's a reasonable part of the forecasting mix and is easy to follow.

Information on temporary worker placement is available from the Department of Labor and is usually reported in newspapers, other news reports and feature stories. Since this indicator is not a strong forecaster, it has no lead time and should only be used to confirm actual leading indicators.

2. Decreased unemployment

Unemployment statistics are not a valid leading indicator, but the fact that the unemployment rate has declined confirms that a recovery is taking place. Decreased unemployment indicates that companies are hiring in order to handle increased business activity and that the economy is gaining strength.

Unemployment relates more to the present, not to the future, and should only be considered as a confirming factor. Check newspapers, other business and financial publications and the Department of Labor for information on decreased unemployment rates.

3. New Orders for Nondefense Capital Goods

The trend in Nondefense Capital Goods New Orders is a good way to measure future business-to-business activity. When orders increase for goods that last more than three years, (such as machinery, vehicles, heavy equipment and conveyor systems), and inventory levels are declining, it verifies the other signs of recovery. New Orders data can be obtained from the Department of Commerce's M3 Publication. The New Orders information provides virtually no lead time.

Invalid indicators

Myths and misinformation are found in every business and industry, but in economic forecasting they abound. The following are indicators that we consider invalid and should not be relied upon.

1. Newspapers and media

Our biggest competitors as forecasters are the Wall Street Journal, the London Financial Times and other respected business and financial publications because people think that what appears in print is gospel, but it's not. Newspapers, even the most prestigious, are not in the business of providing accurate economic forecasts; they're in the business of selling newspapers.

Most print publications have a particular position, point of view or slant that underlies their reporting of the information they provide. To varying degrees, the same holds true with other media outlets: magazines, journals, television, radio, the Internet and blogs. Most have certain positions that they advance.

In days gone by, those who reported the news were considered objective, and most folks felt confident that they could be relied upon. Now that's drastically changed. As the media has expanded, especially on cable and blogs, many outlets have become specialized and more partisan. Many are dedicated to promoting a particular position or point of view. Some are conservative, others liberal, while others fill all levels between. We don't say this to malign these folks in any way; it appears to be either a part of the accepted culture or perhaps even of being human and not automatons from whom complete objectivity should be expected.

In addition, we now have media outlets that specialize in business and finance. And each has spawned pundits who can't wait to tell us their opinions on what tomorrow will bring. It can get confusing because these pundits constantly seem to be disagreeing and often publicly bicker. Many of these media personalities owe their careers more to the facts that they look good and are articulate and entertaining rather than to their forecasting prowess.

So don't rely solely on media forecasts. If their forecasts sound good, verify the information on which it's based before you spring into action.

2. Unemployment

Many people watch unemployment closely and can quote the unemployment rate on a monthly basis. We applaud their sense of civic and economic awareness. However, please understand that, at best, the change in the number of people employed is a coincidental indicator and is always old news. It doesn't help you see the future because unemployment statistics are a product of what occurred in the past, even if it was just yesterday. High employment figures show that the economy was strong at the time those statistics were compiled, but they provide no valid indication of what the future holds.

Looking at unemployment is like driving down a highway with your eyes firmly fixed in the rear-view mirror. You get a great view of where you've been, but absolutely no help seeing the next turn in the road. In fact, it is harmful because looking back distracts you and keeps you from paying attention to where you really want to go!

3. Consumer expectations

Many forecasters give great weight to consumer expectations (sometimes called consumer confidence or consumer sentiment), but it has generally proven to be an invalid leading indicator. For examples of its unreliability, let's look at recent history.

- From 1983 to 1990, consumer confidence was in a prolonged but mildly negative trend, yet retail sales moved higher through this period.

- From 1990 to 2000, consumer confidence vacillated wildly, but a strong, general upward trend took hold and retail sales increased.

- From 2000 to the fourth quarter of 2008 consumer confidence plummeted, but retail sales still rose. The bottom did not fall out for retail sales until autumn 2008.

At no point in time can you look at consumer expectations and say, "I know what consumers will do." The volatility is too great and the public is too quick to respond to whatever news or opinions are on CNN that day.

4. Sales force reports

We often hear, "My sales people tell me," which can be a bottom-up forecasting tool that has some value. Certainly ground intelligence has value and should not be disregarded in getting a handle on how your customers are faring. The problem is that most salespeople are optimists who approach everything, especially selling, in the most favorable light. Their optimism is a major part of their skill set; it motivates them and convinces their customers.

Sales people tend to focus on the here and now, not tomorrow. They're practical individuals who want to quickly close deals and earn their commissions. Most don't look at forecasting factors because they're zeroed in on today. Although they may know how the wind is blowing today, they have no idea if it's going to change.

When you rely on sales people, you're asking your cheerleaders whether the sky will be blue tomorrow. Their answers will virtually always be "yes." Seeing the bright side is their nature, it's their job and it's in their DNA. If you find a pessimistic salesperson, he or she is probably in the wrong career.

5. The pallet index

In the past, it was common to base forecasts on the number of wooden shipping pallets manufactured and sold. Forecasters believed that an increase in pallet construction and sales heralded an economic recovery because it showed that producers were getting ready to ship more goods. When pallet manufacturing and sales declined, the forecasters felt that production and shipping would slow.

The pallet index is no longer a valid leading indicator because wooden pallets are becoming obsolete. As we import more products, wooden pallets are used less frequently.

6. Politicians

Our political figures love to pontificate on the economy and the future. They seem to enjoy nothing more than warning us about what tomorrow may bring and declaring how they can protect us from all the dark forces that lurk beyond. Many believe that government is the solution, and we're frequently left feeling that if it were not for Congress and/ or the Administration in power we would have no hope of competing globally or even of putting food on our tables next year.

More often than not, our politicians' predictions are based on their hopes — or what they think we hope — rather than more concrete, fact-based evidence. Many tell us what we want to hear and promise to provide the monetary solutions that will make us happy once again. Although their words may cheer us up for a while and help get them elected, in reality, their solutions may not address the real problems at hand.

The reality is that the US economy is too large for even Congress to easily manipulate. The economy is much more complicated than most of us can begin to imagine and no one-size-fits-all levers or buttons can create a quick fix. Tinkering with the complex machinery of the economy can lead to some nasty unintended consequences.

MAKE YOUR MOVE >>> A better approach than relying on others is to develop your own solutions. Lead your businesses by:

- Constantly tracking the leading indicators.

- Making plans according to the information the leading indicators reveal.

- Taking the initiative; being proactive — so you won't have to be reactive. Instead of hoping that the tide will turn in your way or that the government will solve your problems, take the helm.

Look to yourself and the leading indicators. Then make your plans and lay the groundwork for the future you want because you are the solution.

Business is a noble endeavor that serves a great purpose. It is the engine that enables our country to thrive. Businesses employ people, they teach them skills and make it possible for them and our nation to be productive. It is the vehicle that lifts hard-working individuals, gives them stature, is the means to great accomplishments, and lets them lead comfortable lives.

ECO-SENSE

While we're mired in this economic downturn and so many of our largest businesses and institutions are on the ropes, the profit motive has been under attack. Profit making has been equated to greed and those who are employed to make profits have fallen into disfavor. Sure, some contemptible individuals have been abusive and leaped way over the line, but their crimes — as unspeakable as they are — certainly don't prove that profit making is corrupt. Take a broader view.

In order to survive, companies must make profits. If they don't, their employees will lose their jobs and production or service activity will stop. If production stopped, we would become dependent on others to fill our needs and lose the dynamic that enabled this country to prosper.

In our system, profits are the time-honored goal and are the cornerstone of our nation's prosperity. However, profits must go hand in hand with ethics because if businesses do not operate under the highest standards, they won't survive. Their brands will be tarnished, and they will be displaced by those who play by the rules.

Remember

Leading indicators signal the phase of the business cycle in which the economy is heading. Take a systematic approach in using leading indicators. Determine which leading indicators fit your business and when any two of them reveal a trend, pay attention and start planning how to deal with that trend. When five leading indicators turn in the same direction, have your resources lined up and be ready to implement your plan because change is on the way.

In addition to leading indicators, confirming indicators exist. Confirming indicators should not be used alone because they are not valid signals that a change in the economy is at hand. However, they are helpful in confirming that a change will be taking place. Learn which commonly accepted indicators are invalid and don't place stock in them.

CLIENT PROFILE: Dupre Transport, Lafayette, Louisiana

- ¬ Founded in 1980 with two trucks, only one of which ran.
- ¬ In 2008, Dupre Transport grossed over $120 million.

OVERALL: ITR® provides a competitive advantage to Dupre because our forecasts allow it to look 3 to 5 years forward when most economists are looking just to their year-end.

METHODOLOGY:

Ongoing

1. Each month, 18 people on Dupre's management team receive EcoTrends®.
2. They read the EcoTrends® summaries and four to five major pages and then explain the relevant information to their key managers. This process has "significantly increased management's economic understanding of reality versus what they hear on the news," according to Doug Place, Dupre's CFO.
3. Dupre's key mangers examine specific indicators identified by ITR® and decide how they apply to their business.

Long-term

Reggie Dupre (CEO), Tom Voelkel (President and COO) and Doug Place (CFO) decided to look into the future and developed a 10-year plan. Each quarter, they compare the company's progress with ITR® data to make sure that they are on target. Specifically, they check to see if they are "way over the bow," discuss wage strategies, business groups and scenario planning.

Dupre holds annual strategic planning meetings that look 3 to 5 years ahead. Using data from ITR®, Dupre also develops assumptions, strategies and the next year's budget. The assumptions relate to revenue, labor increases, fuel costs, inflation and group margin targets.

SPECIFIC BENEFITS

Late Phase B

- In summer 2006, ITR˙ informed Dupre of an impending world oil shortage. Based on that information and our discussions, Dupre speculated in the oil market and made about $1.5 million in two years.

- Discussions that Dupre held in its monthly, quarterly and annual meetings convinced it to sell its underperforming Over-The-Road van unit of 150 trucks in 2007, before the recession we anticipated for the second half of 2008.

- Dupre used our late-2008 and 2009 forecast to time its contracts and avoid having to renegotiate in a down cycle. As a result, all Dupre's contracts are set to expire in 2008, 2011 or 2012 and it has no contracts to renegotiate in 2009.

- In 2007, Dupre made missionary efforts and became involved in the alternative energy market. That segment of the company has grown from 3% to 10% of Dupre's total business (from $4 million to $12 million) and more growth is expected.

- In 2007, Dupre decided against expanding into the warehouse business and the container business, both of which have since tanked. The company also elected not to build a bio-diesel plant, which worked out well since fuel prices have dropped.

- Since working with ITR˙, Dupre has planned its acquisitions according to the phases of the business cycle. It did not make acquisitions in 2007 or 2008 because we forecasted that period would be the top of the business cycle. However, Dupre is now looking to make acquisitions in 2009 and 2010, when we expect greater bargains to be available.

Late Phase D, Early Phase A

- As a defined strategy, Dupre now bases its price increases on the phases of the business cycle. Each quarter, it bases its plans according to where the economy is in the business cycle. For the second and third quarters of 2007, Dupre increased prices 4.7% in its Energy Distribution Services and 7% in its Strategic Capacity Services. It received no significant push back from customers although it tries to be on the leading edge of price increases. Management used ITR® economic data to sell the increases to the sales force before it passed them along to customers.

- Periodically, Dupre determines which phase of the business cycle it's in. Then it refers to our list of Management Objectives™ for that phase and anticipates how each management objective could affect each of its business groups.

Phase C

- In 2008, soaring fuel prices caused many trucking companies to fail. An estimated 90,000 truckers left the industry in the first two quarters alone. Most failed because they did not impose a fuel surcharge or imposed one too late. Not Dupree. Based on information from ITR®, it added a reasonable surcharge and while others failed, Dupre Transport continued to be profitable. "We attribute a lot of our success to being able to look around the corner," Doug Place said "ITR® is interwoven through the fabric of the company."

Chapter 3
Forecasting Tools

The mechanic that would perfect his work must first sharpen his tools.
Confucius

Gold is a favorite topic of investors, economists, industrialists, and governments. You may not know it, but an estimated $6.7 billion worth of gold was mined in the United States in 2008. Thoughts of gold mines in the West bring to mind images of craggy openings held up by rough timber, a trustworthy pack mule, pickaxes and a dusty miner in faded clothes.

Today's mining operations bear little resemblance to those of yesteryear — except for the part of the rugged, risk-taking individual. Miners now risk their capital and their futures in modern operations that utilize the latest technology to maximize ore extraction. That gold ring on your finger is the product of millions of dollars, technologically advanced tools and management know how.

Your endeavor is no different. You are that risk-taking individual looking to extract the most value from your business or organization. The question is, "Are you using the most efficient tools available to accomplish your goals?" In this chapter, we will introduce you to the tools you will need to accomplish your goals as efficiently as possible.

The fundamental process in cyclical analysis is neither complicated nor time consuming. Excel provides an excellent framework for preparing the basic data and then charting it. So let's begin by showing you how to use your data to compute moving totals and rates-of-change.

Data requirements

To determine data trends and rates-of-change, you need sufficient historical data. Your business' historical data is the starting point. We are often asked, "What data should I use?" The answer is twofold.

- First, use data that is readily available. Most of us have kept records of our sales, orders or cash received that we can use. To start, work with whatever is easiest to get your hands on.

- Second, if you have choices in what data to use, examine the metric you are most interested in analyzing. Revenues or sales are the most common, but you can use others including orders, backlog and inventory levels.

Use monthly data for at least a seven-year period because, as a rule, the longer the history, the more accurate the results. Quarterly data can be used if monthly data is not available.

Many firms will also use a separate data stream for their various business segments or major product lines. For instance, how your

OEM sales are faring as distinguished from the figures for your Service Department.

In order to accurately assess your position in the business cycle and to determine when you will be moving through the next turn, your company's raw data must be converted into two tools:

(1) Your 3-month moving total (3MMT)
(2) Your 12-month moving total (12MMT).

These tools form the bedrock upon which the forecasting process is built. Whenever we forecast — whether projecting a company's total sales, product-line sales, some other performance measure or perhaps inflation, exchange rates or the industrial production of a nation — we start by determining the 3MMT and 12MMT.

If a company is enjoying solid growth in sales, as evidenced by a rising trend in its 12MMT, the big question becomes, "How long will its 12MMT rising trend last?" Or stated another way, "When will our 12MMT shift into the next phase of the business cycle?"

Our offer to you

Calculating the 3MMT, 12MMT and the rates-of-change is not difficult, but we would like to simplify the process even further for you. Go to our website at www.ecotrends.org and click on the Make Your Move tab. You will find a fill-in-the-blank template that you are welcome to download and use.

Use column A for the month and year. When you put your data in column B, it will automatically fill in column C. The other columns will automatically be filled in as you enter in enough months of data. The rates-of-change will also be calculated, but let's ignore those for now. The result will look like this:

Example 3-1: Picking up the tools

ABM Corp. Millions of Dollars

	Monthly	1/12	3MMT	3/12	12MMT	12/12
Dec-07	2.529	13.9	7.750	13.7	29.071	0.3
Jan-08	2.564	-2.3	7.517	6.3	29.011	-1.3
Feb-08	2.408	6.0	7.501	5.4	29.148	-0.3
Mar-08	2.516	6.3	7.488	3.1	29.296	1.5
Apr-08	2.787	31.5	7.711	14.1	29.964	4.2
May-08	2.554	11.0	7.857	15.7	30.217	5.5
Jun-08	2.592	9.1	7.933	16.7	30.433	7.0
Jul-08	2.396	10.1	7.542	10.1	30.653	8.1
Aug-08	2.488	3.3	7.476	7.4	30.732	8.9
Sep-08	2.511	-6.2	7.395	1.8	30.566	8.6
Oct-08	2.349	-16.0	7.348	-6.8	30.118	5.4
Nov-08	1.868	-22.9	6.728	-14.8	29.562	2.8
Dec-08	1.784	-29.5	6.001	-22.6	28.817	-0.9
Jan-09	1.608	-37.3	5.260	-30.0	27.861	-4.0
Feb-09	1.524	-36.7	4.916	-34.5	26.977	-7.4
Mar-09	1.623	-35.5	4.755	-36.5	26.084	-11.0
Apr-09	1.418	-49.1	4.565	-40.8	24.715	-17.5

Monthly moving totals

Moving totals are the sum of the monthly total data for a stated number of months. For example, the 3MMT for November would be the sum of the September, October, and November monthly data. When December data becomes available, September is dropped from the calculation and December added. By doing so, the December 3MMT consists of the activity recorded in October, November and December.

Example 3-2: ABM Corp's Sales 3MMT (in millions of $)

January	2009	1.608
February	2009	1.524
March	2009	1.623
	3MMT =	4.755

ABM Corp., a fictional company whose data appears in Example 3-2, had a 3MMT for March 2009 of $4.775 million. April's Sales came in at $1.418 million, making the April 2009 3MMT $4.565 million (February + March + April).

We use moving monthly totals to smooth out the volatility inherent in the data for a particular month or months. 3MMTs are used to illustrate *the seasonal changes* inherent to the data series. They are also used to *forecast specific product activity* on a quarterly basis.

Annual moving totals

Annual moving totals (12MMT) go one step further by looking beyond *seasonal* changes in the data series being collected. They allow us to provide a more accurate overall picture for spotting and forecasting *cyclical trends*.

The 12MMT depicts the sum of activity for 12 consecutive months. For April 2009, it would be the total derived when adding the figures for March 2008 through April 2009. As the data for each new month becomes available, add it and drop the oldest amount.

In our Example 3-1, above, the April 2009 12MMT is arrived at by adding the April 2009 monthly figure ($1.418) to the March 2009 12MMT ($26.084), and then subtracting the April 2008 number ($2.787) from the subtotal. When we refer to a data trend at ITR®, we are referring to the 12MMT trend.

At times, it's desirable to calculate a 12-month moving average (12MMA) instead of a total (12MMTs). Use 12MMAs when it is more logical to think of the data being measured and forecasted in averages. For instance, we don't think of percentages in terms of their total for the last three months, but in terms of their monthly average. The same is true for prices. It makes more sense to find out how much the average price of a commodity will be in the future than to determine what the total commodity price will be in that same period of time. 12MMAs work best with indexes, percentages (for interest rates or inflation) or inventories.

A 12MMA is calculated in the same way as the 12MMT, but with an added step — the 12MMT is divided by 12 to reflect the monthly average for the preceding year. A 12MMA will look exactly like a 12MMT when plotted on a chart. A 3MMA is simply calculating a 3MMT and dividing it by 3.

Rate-of-change:

The 3/12 and 12/12 rates-of-change are the tools that have replaced the gold miner's pickaxe. They are your tools for getting the gold.

Before we dig into the 3/12 and 12/12 rates-of-change, let's begin with the 1/12 rate-of-change. Many firms already use a 1/12 rate-of-change to a limited extent. They compare their sales for the current month with their sales for the same month a year earlier. Management may see that their sales in December 2009 were 6.0% below their sales during December 2008. We don't add much complexity to that basic formula when we discuss the 3/12 and 12/12 rates-of-change. What interests us most is *the direction* in which these rates-of-change are taking us.

Rate-of-change comparisons are utilized for:
- Finding where we are in the business cycle
- Anticipating where we will be in the future

- Seeing how we are performing in relationship to our markets and industry

- Using the leading indicators to help guide us through the changes ahead

- Understanding where we are in our company or product's life cycle.

A 12/12 rate-of-change, which is discussed below, is more sensitive to changes in cyclical status and momentum than is the 12MMT. It also can be successfully used to anticipate trend reversals, often before the data trend even begins to show signs of weakening or even better, before the data trend shows signs of strengthening from a recession.

Keep in mind that the timing estimates for rates-of-change give us valuable insights into inflection points in data trends. Ultimately, we want to know when the data trend is going to reach a low and then begin to rise or when it will reach a high and then descend. The rate of rise or decline that we see in the rate-of-change is often indicative of how steep or mild the recovery or recession will be. Usually, the rate-of-change reflects a change in a data trend before the change becomes apparent in either the 3MMT or 12MMT.

Calculating Rate-of-Change

A rate-of-change figure is the ratio (the simple percentage) of a number in a data series to a preceding number in that data series. When calculating the rates-of-change, the time interval between the numbers being compared is fixed. One rate-of-change figure can tell you instantly whether activity is running below or above this time last year, and by how much.

When rates-of-change move consecutively in the same direction, it indicates that activity levels are getting *progressively* better or worse compared to last year. The rate-of-change of a data series illustrates and measures *cyclical* change and identifies *trends*. The 12/12 rate-of-change is also key to finding important relationships to leading indicators that will enable you to see down into that mineshaft to the gold below.

The most common rate-of-change is the 12/12. As is the case for all rates-of-change, the numerator (upper number in the fraction) denotes how much data is involved. In Example 3-1, the April 2009 12MMT for ABM Corp's sales was $24.715 million.

When calculating the 12/12 rate-of-change, the upper 12 (numerator) of the 12/12 specifies that a 12MMT comparison is being made. The lower 12 (denominator) signifies that the time interval is 12 months (for all of our work represented by this text, the time interval will be fixed at 12 months). The 12/12 rate-of-change for April 2009, expressed as a percent, would be calculated as follows:

Example 3-3:

$$\left[\left(\frac{April\ 2009\quad 12MMT\quad 24.715}{April\ 2008\quad 12MMT\quad 29.964}\right)\times\ 100\right] - 100\ =\ -17.5\%\quad April\ 2009\quad 12/12$$

The April 2009 12MMT was 17.5% below the April 2008 12MMT.

In our hypothetical case, a positive result is also possible

Example 3-4:

$$\left[\left(\frac{April\ 2010\quad 12MMT\quad 27.112}{April\ 2009\quad 12MMT\quad 24.715}\right)\times\ 100\right] - 100\ =\ +9.7\%\quad April\ 2010\quad 12/12$$

The 9.7% rate-of-change figure reflects the fact that ABM Corp's activity for the 12 months ending April 2010 is 9.7% above the level of activity it posted for the 12 months ending April 2009. The 12/12 provides a snapshot as of a given month. It shows where ABM stands today in relation to its annual total of one year ago. The essential question in forecasting future change is whether this figure is trending upward or downward. Identifying the direction of the 12/12 trend begins to give definition to where a company is in the business cycle.

ECO-SENSE

At ITR˚, our research has shown that a business cycle change can be more accurately observed, measured, and forecasted using rates-of-change as opposed to the actual data.

Another rate-of-change frequently used in measuring cyclical change is the 3/12. As the numerator indicates, the figures being compared are 3MMTs. The time interval is 12 months. The 3/12 rate-of-change is not used to define the business cycle of the data series per se, but as a tool to better enable us to anticipate shifts in the business cycle trend. ABM Corp's 3/12 is calculated as follows:

Example 3-5:

$$\left[\left(\frac{April\ 2009\ \ 3MMT\ \ \ 4.565}{April\ 2008\ \ 3MMT\ \ \ 7.711} \right) \times\ 100 \right] - 100\ =\ -40.8\%\quad April\ 2009\ \ 3/12$$

ABM's sales for the 3 months ending April 2009 were down 40.8% from the year before. To gauge the business cycle momentum, monitor your data to see if this figure is improving, approaching 0.0%, or decreasing, falling further below -40.8%. The 3/12 and the 12/12 are the two most frequently used rates-of-change when analyzing company or market data.

At times, the 1/12 rate-of-change should be employed for aggregate, macroeconomic data series which are not prone to significant swings from one month to the next. Dividing the most recent monthly figure by the monthly figure a year ago will give you the 1/12 rate-of-change. Be careful with the 1/12 because it can be too volatile for use at the company level. ABM Corp's 1/12 is calculated as follows:

Example 3-6:

$$\left[\left(\frac{April\ 2009\quad monthly\ data\quad 1.418}{April\ 2008\quad monthly\ data\quad 2.787}\right) \times 100\right] - 100 = -49.1\% \quad April\ 2009\quad 1/12$$

As this example shows, ABM's business is down 49.1% from this same time a year ago. What we need to know next is whether this figure is part of an ongoing downward trend or whether it could reflect that some improvement has begun in the company's position in the business cycle. To find the answer, we will need to find out how the 1/12 is relating to the 3/12 and 12/12 rates-of-change.

The 12/12 rate-of-change shows where a company is in the business cycle and when its cyclical status will change. According to our research, using the rate-of-change, rather than the actual data, provides more accurate analysis and forecast results. Trend characteristics related to timing and dynamics can be more easily observed, measured, and utilized for anticipating what lies ahead for the company.

In Chapter 4, we will use the relationship of the 3/12 to the 12/12 to gain insight into the current business cycle status and the future trend probabilities for the 12/12 rate-of-change. For now, let's stay focused on just the 12/12 rate-of-change.

Knowing your phase

When you navigate on land or sea or air, you need to know where you are before you can chart an effective course to your destination. When we work with our client companies, we are in the same position. We need to know what phase of the cycle they are currently in so we can use our Management Objectives™ most effectively to maximize our clients' profitability and to make sure they stay in the growth portion of the cycle for as long as possible.

You would be amazed at how often we're told, "My company has always grown." We always reply, "Great!" However, we then ask:

- What is your rate of growth?
- Does it vary over time? (It normally does).
- Have you been in business during a really tough period for the economy?

Growing is awesome, but you need to know (1) if your rate of growth is accelerating or decelerating and (2) how your movement relates to what the economic indicators are telling us about the future.

ALAN SAYS

"Setting your sails correctly involves more than staying in your cabin and knowing the ship is going forward". The reality is that the longer you go forward *without* making changes, such as coming out of your cabin and adjusting the trim of your sails, the more likely it is that your ship will end up on the rocks!

You can use two methods to determine what phase of the cycle you're passing through. Both utilize the 12/12 rate-of-change. You can use an Excel or other spreadsheet and work from the numbers. Or you can make a chart showing your rates-of-change. Some folks like the visuals — others want just the numbers. Either method will let you see the phase of the cycle you're passing though and where you're headed.

MAKE YOUR MOVE>>> When you have calculated your 12/12 rate-of-change, step back, and look at the numbers. Begin with the most recent results and answer the following questions:

1. Is the 12/12 becoming less negative (heading toward zero)? You are in Phase A.
2. Is the 12/12 climbing higher and higher above zero? Welcome to Phase B. Enjoy!
3. Is the 12/12 greater than zero but slipping lower? You are passing through Phase C.
4. Is the 12/12 less than zero and the number is getting worse? That would be Phase D and it is time we get out of there!

If you are the visual type, use the Excel function for charting your data. Create a chart with separate lines for the 3/12 and the 12/12 rates-of-change. If you have a lot of history, confine yourself to the last seven years. The four questions presented above now apply to you.

Checking in

Example 3-1 shows that ABM Corp's sales for the 12 months ending April 2009 reached $24.715 million and a quick 12/12 computation shows that so far 2009 is coming in 17.5% below 2008 through a comparable period. As you will soon see, the fact that the 3/12 is even weaker at -40.8% (Example 3-5) is an ominous sign for ABM Corp.'s near-term trend probabilities.

The 12/12 rate-of-change becomes even more important when you compare ABM Corp. to the industry trends. ABM's -17.5% growth rate may not be so bad if its industry declined by 24.3%!

ECO-SENSE

It's not unusual for a company to experience more up and down swings than its industry or market benchmarks. So if you have a 6.0% decline when the market slipped by 12.3%, it may be quite an accomplishment. Your results may reflect a difference in your market share from the beginning to the end of the period, a change in your product mix or differing price movement. Whatever the reason, enjoy it because it means you beat the market!

Rate-of-change trend

The trend in the 12/12 rate-of-change is important. ABM Corp's 12/12 values from September 2008 through April 2009 came in at 8.6%, 5.4%, 2.8%, -0.9%, -4.0%, -7.4%, -11.0% and -17.5%. It would look like this if charted on a simple line chart.

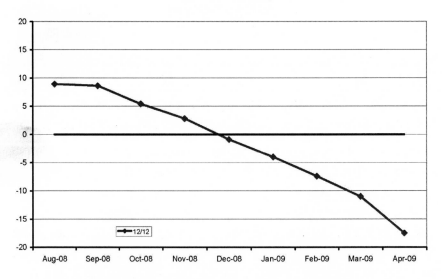

Chart 3-7: Trend in 12/12 Rate–of-Change.

The numbers show that ABM's rate of growth went from slowing (12/12 above 0) to contraction (12/12 dropping further below 0). We now need to determine how long that 12/12 will continue its downward movement. We have several means at our disposal.

BRIAN SAYS

You can change your future, if you (1) see what your trend is likely to be based on leading indicators and (2) know what is normal for your company. Think a half business cycle ahead.

How can you avoid negative year-over-year comparisons before they arrive? If you wait until you're in the thick of a trend before you try to change the outcome, you will probably be too late. Too many failed companies said, "If sales get soft, we'll take X, Y, and Z actions." They were too late. Be vigilant and become a student of change and of business cycles to make sure you never see those negative year-over-year comparisons!

How long?

Knowing where your company is now is important to accountants and folks concerned with today's output, inventory needs and cash requirements. Knowing where your company is _going_ is the stuff of strategists, planners and forecasters.

Answer the following questions in order to determine how long a 12/12 trend will last.

- What is normal?
- Are there internal indications of cyclical change?
- How do I compare to industry trends and what are those trends telling me?
- How do I relate to leading indicators and what are they signaling?

In this chapter, we will tackle the first question, "What is normal?" and the other three will be covered in subsequent chapters.

When we use the term "normal," we mean what is typical, customary, or standard for your specific company, industry or markets. ABM Corp's 12/12 rate-of-change has been moving lower from its August 2008 high. Hang onto that thought because we will get back to it. Now take the following steps:

1. *Rank the downward trend.* A look at all of ABM's previous 12/12 declining trends shows that five earlier declines lasted 21, 12, 15, 19 and 13 months respectively. Let's rank them in descending order:

21   19   15   13   12

2. *Determine the centered majority range.* The centered majority of five cases is three. The three center cases are 19, 15 and 13, which means that ABM Corp's 12/12 rate-of-change will probably fall for 13 to 19 months. The median length of decline should be 15 months. When applied to its August 2008 12/12 high, it would be normal for ABM's 12/12 to descend to between September 2009 and March 2010 and the median length of decline would result in an October 2009 12/12 low.

Determine the centered majority range by first finding the simple majority for the data set and then drop off an even number of extreme cases from consideration. The centered majority of a hypothetical sample containing seven observations would be four, but the extreme cases would total three. Eliminating three extremes will not work because we need an even number of extremes to keep the equation *centered*. Since four doesn't work, we must try five as the centered majority. Five works because we end up dropping one extreme case from either end. When an even number of extremes has been eliminated from consideration, the majority of the sample remains intact.

The determination of the centered majority range and the median works the same way for an even number of cases. Let's take the above case and expand it to eight previous declines.

24   21   19   18   15   15   13   12

The simple majority of eight is five, but five does not work because we need to drop an even number of cases from each end (eight minus five is three and we need an even number). We must move up to six as the majority range and drop one case from each end. The majority range length of decline is now 13 to 21 with the median length of decline at 17 (the average of the two middle cases, 18 and 15, rounded up to the nearest whole number). A median (typical) length of decline off the August 2008 high would result in a 12/12 low in January 2010.

The same computation should be done for rising trends as well.

3. *Keep "normal" current.* Annually revisit the lengths of rise and/or decline to see if the majority range and median estimates have shifted. It will only take a few minutes and it will help avoid timing drifts.

12/12 rate-of-change trends are not always smooth. They don't always have easy to determine shifts from rise to decline or decline to rise. Knowing what is normal will give you confidence as to the sustainability of a tentative cyclical shift. Your confidence level will also be boosted when you learn how to use the Checking Points that we discuss in the next chapter, Ch. 4.

Rates-of-change vs. actual data

Rate-of-change can also be used as a stand-alone tool in the forecasting and decision making process. However, frequently a rate-of-change percentage figure must be translated back into a formula that reveals *when* the data trend will reverse direction.

The process begins by:

1. Measuring the timing relationship between 12/12 rate-of-change cyclical lows and corresponding 12MMT data trend recession lows that have historically occurred
2. The same observation must be conducted between 12/12 rate-of-change highs and data trend peaks
3. Rank your findings and determine the median (typical) and majority range (normal) parameters.

ABM Corp.'s 12/12 will typically lead the 12MMT through a low by zero months with a majority range of zero to two months. Determining a timing estimate for the 12/12 becomes crucial in this case because ABM's sales 12MMT will begin to rise about the same time as the 12/12 rate-of-change and the company will not want to be caught flat-footed, waiting for a recovery that has in fact already begun! Our analysis shows that a 12/12 rate-of-change high means that ABM typically has one to two quarters before the data trend reverses direction and begins to turn down.

It is often important to relate probable shifts in the direction of a 3MMT trend to the anticipated timing of a 12/12-trend reversal. For a highly seasonal series (such as housing starts or many retail related industries), the seasonal low occurring prior to the anticipated 12/12 low will be the *cyclical* turning point as well as the seasonal low. The seasonal high in the 3MMT transpiring either just before or immediately after the 12/12 peak will also often be the *cyclical* apex for the 3MMT.

MAKE YOUR MOVE>>> If the data series is not highly seasonal:

- Measure the time interval between corresponding 3MMT cyclical trend reversals and 12/12 trend reversal (matching lows to lows and highs to highs)
- Rank the resulting time intervals as was done for the 12MMTs
- Determine the median (typical) and majority range (normal) timing relationships.

In this manner, a projected 12/12 trend reversal can be translated into the probable reversal for the 3MMT. Of course, the same calculations could be performed for the actual monthly data if desired.

Remember

You can know with a high degree of confidence when your company will transition from rise to decline or decline to rise by using the rate-of-change methodology. Calculating timing relationships and utilizing Checking Points enhances the process and will take you from "it would be normal" to "I am quite confident that…"

In addition, you can also accurately make short-term forecasts based on what is happening inside your company. As you do, your bosses, colleagues and associates will be amazed at your ability to see around the corner while they are left to wonder, hope, and suppose about forthcoming changes. It will raise your profile and advance your career.

When you know what phase of the cycle you are in, the other tools that follow will help you determine where you are going. Or should we say, "Where you may be going." After all, where you go ultimately depends on your imagination and the level of energy you bring to bear in order to beat the business cycle.

CHAPTER 4
CHECKING POINTS

History is a cyclic poem written by Time upon the memories of man.

Percy Bysshe Shelley

How would you like an easy-to-read visual aid that will help you (1) determine where your company is in the business cycle and (2) increase your confidence in where it's heading? It would be like having both a GPS and a crystal ball on your dashboard to tell you exactly where you're going in the short and long term.

The underlying principle in economic forecasting is that changes normally come incrementally and then add up to something more noticeable. As changes occur, they may not be apparent to you. Then all of a sudden, you spot differences.

To help you forecast upcoming changes, we've devised a system of Checking Points. Our Checking Points are similar to the checklist every pilot completes before taking off. Our Checking Points will list each step you must execute before you get off the ground. They will help you make sure that you are ready to go and that everything you need is in place. Then you can take and stay on the most direct route to your destination.

The system of Checking Points we devised at ITR˙ makes it possible to:

A. Better monitor and understand where you are in the current business cycle
B. Identify forthcoming shifts in the business cycle
C. Become more proactive in changing the internal and external forces that affect your business.

Our Checking Point system involves the comparison of either 1/12 or 3/12 rate-of-change trends with the 12/12 rate-of-change. In most cases, a 3/12 to 12/12 comparison should be used. The 3/12 is preferable because the short duration of the 1/12 can give false signals.

Positive and negative points

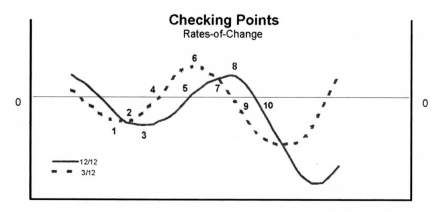

Chart 4-1: Example of Checking Points, Rates-of-Change

As you can see from Chart 4-1, rates-of-change move in both a positive (up) and negative (down) direction. They go above and below the 0 center line. As they do, numbers appear that describe the activity that is taking place. This activity is explained below. Since some of the activity occurs in concert, those Checking Points are described together.

Positive Checking Points

1. 3/12 low
2. 3/12 rises to a level above the 12/12 (upward passing)
3. 12/12 reaches a low
4. 3/12 crosses above the 0 line
5. 12/12 crosses above the 0 line

Negative Checking Points

6. 3/12 reaches a high
7. 3/12 downward passes the 12/12
8. 12/12 reaches a high
9. 3/12 crosses below the 0 line
10. 12/12 crosses below the 0 line

Checking Points 1 and 2

The first two points are the earliest empirical indications that ABM Corp. is approaching a 12/12-business cycle low. Checking Point #2, (the 3/12 rate-of-change upward passing) is an important confirming indication that the cyclical momentum will soon be shifting from negative to positive. An upward passing occurs when ABM's 3/12 activity literally moves above its 12/12.

- o Checking Point 1 gives hope
- o Checking Point 2 brings downright excitement
- o With Checking Points 1 and 2 behind you, your engines are fired up because you can see that business is rolling down the runway about to lift off.

Use the historical relationship between ABM Corp's 3/12 and its 12/12 to determine the probable timing for the 12/12 low (actual liftoff!).

- Review your data history and measure the length of interval of time in months between the time when the 3/12 passed through each sustained low and when a corresponding 12/12 low was established.

- Rank your findings to determine the median and centered majority range lead/lag timing relationship between a 3/12 low and a corresponding 12/12 low, as discussed in Chapter 3.

Ranking simply involves listing your findings in order from the longest lead-time (in months) to the shortest lead-time.

$$9 \ 7 \ 6 \ 5 \ 4 \ 4 \ 3 \ 3 \ 1 \ 0$$

The median of a ranked series is the middle number. Since we have 10 cases, the median is calculated by averaging the middle two numbers, which are both 4. So our median is four months. That means that the 3/12 rate-of-change will, on median, precede the 12/12 through a business cycle low by four months. In the absence of data to the contrary, a median relationship should be considered the most probable occurrence.

As you will recall from Chapter 3, the majority range is derived by excluding the extreme values from the set of numbers and keeping the centered majority of figures within the set. What is left is the *majority range* result of 3-6 months. The majority range defines *normal behavior*. For example, it would be normal for the 12/12 rate-of-change to pass through a business cycle low three to six months after the 3/12 has passed through a low.

Checking Point 3

At Checking Point 3, the 12/12 rate-of-change has actually established a low for the current business cycle. The reversal of the 12/12 signifies an official end to the cyclical downturn and the beginning of the business cycle's anticipated rising trend, which will consist of recovery and growth.

- o   Checking Point 3 tells us that better days are ahead. Our business is airborne once again!

This shift in business cycle momentum and direction tells you that important decisions must be made regarding your business. The nature of these decisions will be presented later in this book.

Checking Points 4 and 5

Points 4 and 5 are monitoring Checking Points. The 3/12 upward crossing (moving above zero) signifies that quarterly activity is now running above the level of a year ago. The 12/12 upward crossing indicates that the annual moving total is now higher than it was at this time last year.

- o   We are gaining altitude. The sky is the limit for now.

ECO-SENSE

Like a plane flying from New York to LA, your business isn't going to keep rising at an accelerating pace forever. Unless you continuously buy other firms or routinely introduce new services or products that are equally well received, the rate of rise for your business will level off. Your next goal must be to keep the business flying at as high an altitude as possible for as long as possible.

Checking Point 6

Checking Points 6 and 7 are based on the realization that rising trends do not last forever and that it's possible to anticipate a business cycle high because the rate of increase (rate of rise) in the actual data will taper off as the data trend moves toward its eventual peak. This slowing of the rate of increase will be reflected first by Checking Point 6 — the 3/12 rate-of-change high.

> o   When Checking Point 6 occurs, your first thought should be, "What is the next something 'new' that will bring us to an even higher altitude?"

Checking Point 7

This is an important confirming indication that the rate of growth is at best stabilizing, but more likely progressing in a normal cyclical manner toward slower and slower growth. Eventually, this trend may lead to an actual business cycle decline.

> o   Unless you do something amazing, you will be counting down to a diminishing rate of growth.

Utilize the 3/12 to 12/12 timing relationship through business cycle highs in the same manner as we previously outlined for business cycle lows. You should:

1.   Measure the historical timing relationships between 3/12 peaks and the corresponding 12/12 peaks
2.   Rank the data
3.   Calculate the median and majority range parameters.

Checking Point 8

When the 12/12 rate-of-change establishes a business cycle high, you are at Checking Point 8. The 12/12 high signifies that the strongest rate of rise for this business cycle is now behind you. When the data trend progressively decelerates, a recession is now likely.

BRIAN SAYS

The period immediately following Checking Point 8 is arguably the most dangerous Phase of the business cycle. You are still flying high. At first, your business' rate of growth is just barely decelerating. Cash is good and profits are getting even better. What's not to love?

---

o   The issue is (1) whether you're on a glide path to a soft landing where you will just be slow in coming back to earth or (2) will the economic engines soon cut out on you? Leading indicators will provide important clues and the Checking Points will provide hard data.

Checking Points 9 and 10

Our final Checking Points refer to the time when the 3/12 and the 12/12 rates-of-change move below the 0 line. A recession is now in place.

o   The economic engines are sputtering. This downturn could have devastating results for our business.

The level of activity on a quarterly basis (Checking Point 9) and/or on a 12MMT basis (Checking Point 10) is running below the levels of a year ago. From this point forward through the duration of the business cycle, look for an inevitable slowing of the rate of recession. It will be a prelude to a cyclical low and subsequent recovery.

Initially, you will see the deceleration in the rate of recession at the advent of Checking Point 1. The 3/12 rate-of-change will hit a low followed by the 3/12 moving up and passing the 12/12 (Checking Point 2). The process will then begin again and will typically span a period of 3½ to 4 years.

Going beyond

One of the most enjoyable things about our job is that we meet a lot of people with graphs Sometimes they have lots of graphs. We love them and look at their graphs as if they are works of art (you already know economists are a bit different, don't you?). The reason we see lots of graphs is pretty simple. Once you begin the process of forecasting where sales are headed, you will want to apply it to all aspects of business.

MAKE YOUR MOVE>>> Use the process described in Chapters 3 and 4 to track, analyze and forecast the trends for other parts of your business including your gross profits, accounts receivables, division performance, store performance, product lines and anything else of interest to your firm. Excel makes it easy to keep these graphs current and your internal dashboard will light up when you start getting the hang of this proven way of looking at your business.

Share your information with your management team on a regular basis. The more that they "hear the music" the more likely it is that they will sing along when you describe upcoming changes to meet the changing economic environment.

Remember

You can determine with a high degree of confidence when your company will transition from rise to decline or decline to rise by using the rate-of-change methodology presented in Chapter 3 and the verification system we outlined in this chapter. Calculating timing relationships and utilizing checking points will enhance the process and take you from "it would be normal" to "I am quite confident that…"

Now you can accurately forecast what the future holds for your company for the short term. Your bosses, colleagues and employees will be amazed at your ability to see around the corner while they are left to wonder, hope and guess about forthcoming changes. Your new knowledge will strengthen your position in your company and in your industry.

As we move to Chapter 5, we will be looking outside the confines of company data to examine external trends that will enable you to do longer-term forecasting.

NOW WOULD BE A GOOD TIME...

Now is an ideal time to put this book down, go to our website, **www. ecotrends.org**, and have someone on your staff track your sales or other important facets of your business. If you assign the task to someone else, he or she will probably complete it by the time you finish reading Chapter 5. If you have your tracking information available when you start to read Chapter 6, it will enable you to do longer-term forecasting with your own data.

Don't forget to get the majority range and median timing estimates described above. They are key to learning the shorter-term outlook for your business. They will also boost your confidence as to when the current economic conditions will begin to change.

Soon, we will be discussing the four phases of the business cycle and the psychology associated with each phase. Knowing where you are in the business cycle is an important first step toward managing the future and will be easy once you have worked through Chapters 3 and 4. Then you can take on the challenges of managing the changes that lie ahead, including attitudinal changes that must be made in the different phases.

The process we have embarked on is called Trendcast™ here at ITR˙. This is a process by which we take your data and find which leading indicators work the best for you. We then determine where you are in the business cycle and when you will be moving through the next peak or trough, depending on circumstances. The research is followed up by an in-depth discussion with your leadership team. It is at that time that we discuss which moves might be best for you.

CHAPTER 5
A SYSTEM FOR SEEING INTO THE FUTURE

Nine-tenths of wisdom is being wise in time.

Theodore Roosevelt

September 2007: ABM is holding its strategic planning meeting. The corporate leaders are putting together a three-year budget that encompasses sales goals, costs, and capital requirements. The economy is strong and the stock market is doing very well. Although there have been some rumblings about housing, the company takes solace from knowing it is not in the housing market; and, perhaps best of all, the experts — including the Federal Reserve Board — are signaling that all systems will be on 'go' for the next few years. Sales are projected to grow by 10% in 2008, 12% in 2009, and 12% in 2010.

September 2008: ABM's management team meets and affirms last year's projections. In 2007, revenues reached $29.1 million, and management expects ABM's sales to jump by 12% in 2008 (beating previous expectations by two percent), with similar growth in 2009 and 2010. Everyone feels good — optimistic about the future! Some concerns exist that the economy might be faltering, but ABM's sales force is upbeat because ABM is performing better than the economy! The future looks bright: sales are projected to grow to $32.6 million by the end of 2008, $36.5 million for 2009, and $40.9 million in 2010. Plus, everyone expects the bottom line to improve. Life is good.

September 2009: The mood at ABM's strategic planning meeting is somber. Intense discussions center on reducing the work force, cutting costs, and generating operating cash. ABM missed its target for 2008 when its sales faltered late in the third quarter and then tumbled sharply during the last quarter. No one can remember such a quick precipitous drop. And the numbers for the first three quarters of 2009 aren't any better. The latest estimates suggest that yearly sales will be $17.9 million, down 37.9% from 2008 and 51.0% below the estimate the leadership affirmed a year ago.

What happened? The economy went sour and everyone at ABM is saying, "Nobody could have seen it coming." "There was nothing we could do."

Don't believe it, not even for a moment.

You can see changes in the economy coming and gauge their impact on your business before they occur. In this chapter, we will show you exactly what to do.

We know it is possible because that is what we do! That's why, over a year before the recession started, in our January 2007 monthly EcoTrends® report we proclaimed the following:

Our analysis suggests that we are still on track for a recession beginning in 2008 and extending through 2009.

It's in the data

Forecasting is all in the data, in knowing what data to use, and how to look at it.

The process of determining the impact that the economy is likely to have on your business may seem daunting, but it's really a straightforward process. Basically, it breaks down into four steps. Here's what you have to do:

1. Compute your rate-of-change
2. Compare your rate-of-change to macro (general) and industry trends
3. Calculate your timing relationships to leading indicators
4. Complete the Timing Analysis Table

Let's examine these four steps individually using our ABM Corp. to illustrate how the process works. ABM is a conglomerate that has direct and distributor sales throughout the US in a number of different industries. It has been in business for 30 years and has been quite successful. However, as of late, ABM has been hammered by the recession and by its vulnerability to changes in consumer spending. Naturally ABM would like to avoid a repeat in the future if it can.

Here is what ABM Corp must do:

Step one – Compute the rate-of-change

We presented this process in Chapter 3. It is a critical first step, so review that material if necessary.

You can go to our website at www.ecotrends.org and look for the Economic Data navigation button; click it, and then click "rate-of-change template" if you need a starting point for entering your data. The template is an Excel file that will have the months down the left side of the sheet and the heading across the top that you saw in Chapter 3 and from the example below.

Template 5-1

	Monthly	1/12	3MMT	3/12	12MMT	12/12
			ABM Corp Millions of $			
Dec-07						
Jan-08						
Feb-08						
Mar-08						
Apr-08						

More important than the particular spread sheet you use is what data you select for analysis. At least at first, utilize the data that reflects the primary means of looking at the company, such as your gross sales, or revenues, or shipments. The results will look like Example 5-2 below.

Example 5-2

	Monthly	1/12	3MMT	3/12	12MMT	12/12
			ABM Corp Millions of $			
Dec-07	2.529	13.9	7.750	13.7	29.071	0.3
Jan-08	2.564	-2.3	7.517	6.3	29.011	-1.3
Feb-08	2.408	6.0	7.501	5.4	29.148	-0.3
Mar-08	2.516	6.3	7.488	3.1	29.296	1.5
Apr-08	2.787	31.5	7.711	14.1	29.964	4.2
May-08	2.554	11.0	7.857	15.7	30.217	5.5
Jun-08	2.592	9.1	7.933	16.7	30.433	7.0
Jul-08	2.396	10.1	7.542	10.1	30.653	8.1
Aug-08	2.488	3.3	7.476	7.4	30.732	8.9
Sep-08	2.511	-6.2	7.395	1.8	30.566	8.6
Oct-08	2.349	-16.0	7.348	-6.8	30.118	5.4

ABM Corp Millions of $

	Monthly	1/12	3MMT	3/12	12MMT	12/12
Nov-08	1.868	-22.9	6.728	-14.8	29.562	2.8
Dec-08	1.784	-29.5	6.001	-22.6	28.817	-0.9
Jan-09	1.608	-37.3	5.260	-30.0	27.861	-4.0
Feb-09	1.524	-36.7	4.916	-34.5	26.977	-7.4
Mar-09	1.623	-35.5	4.755	-36.5	26.084	-11.0
Apr-09	1.418	-49.1	4.565	-40.8	24.715	-17.5

Computing ABM Corp's Rate-of-Change

Once you have run your company data through the spreadsheet, follow the other steps we explained in Chapter 3 to compute the 12/12 rate-of-change normal length of rise and the normal length of decline (See Determining the Center Majority Range). In Chapter 3, we saw that ABM Corp's 12/12 rate-of-change normally declines from 13 to 21 months and that its typical length of decline is 17 months.

Since ABM's 12/12 high occurred in August 2008 (see example 5-2), the negative trend can typically be expected to bottom out 17 months later, or in January 2010 (based on ABM's typical length of decline). At this point, you have learned when the low might occur. Later in this chapter we will be looking at steps to give us greater confidence in this initial estimate. When we are done, the knowledge will put you well ahead of your competition because you have plausible reasons to expect a recovery in 2010 long before they have a clue.

ECO-SENSE

It may seem like a lot of work to initially compute the 12/12 lengths of rise and then chart the lengths of decline, but the effort will be well worth it. Since new data seldom has to be added (in the above example, a new case needs to be added about every 1½ years), the process will be easy to maintain.

Before we move on to Step Two, note the following information because we will be using it later.

In Chapter 4, we learned how to determine the ABM Corp 3/12 to 12/12 timing relationships for cyclical lows and for cyclical highs. The results:

- It is normal for the ABM Corp 3/12 to lead its 12/12 through *highs* by zero to four months with a median of two months.
- It's also normal for ABM's 3/12 to lead its 12/12 through *lows* by two to seven months and for it to have a median lead of six months.

Step Two – Comparing macro and industry trends using rates-of-change

This step tells you if the changes you're experiencing are in sync with (A) the general economy and (B) your industry or markets. It will show whether you are leading or lagging behind the economy or your industry or markets, or if you are indifferent to changes in them. Start ups, certain niche companies, and companies in acyclical industries tend to be indifferent to the larger environment. Acyclical industries, which we will discuss in Chapter 11, include the pet industry, the medical industry, aspects of the green movement, and global climate change industries.

If ABM is moving in conjunction with the larger economic environment, it can start to plan to make changes in a timely and effective manner. Since we already have the data for ABM (See Chapter 3), now we just need to quantify the macro trend relationship. At least initially, quantify the timing relationship using US Industrial Production, which is available from the Federal Reserve Board, **www.frb.gov**, publication G.17, or on our website (**www.ecotrends.org**) under the Economic Data navigation button.

ABM Corp then prepared a line chart that compared ABM's 12/12 to the US Industrial Production 12/12. It yielded the comparison you see on Chart 5-3.

Chart 5-3

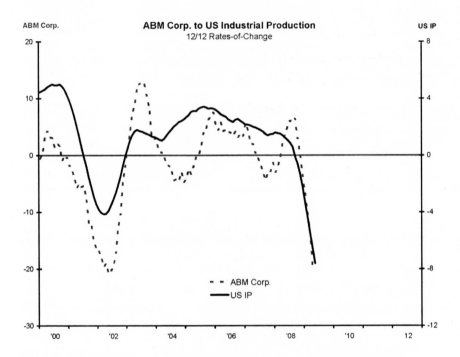

Chart 5-3 shows that changes in the US economy have a bearing on ABM. In order to look forward, ABM's management team must now examine the larger environment to understand what is happening to ABM owing to external forces. ABM can use a credible forecast of US Industrial Production and employ it to forecast when the company will be moving through the upcoming business cycle trough or high. All you need to know is the timing of the US Industrial Production 12/12 trend reversals and how ABM has historically compared to earlier US Industrial Production trend reversals. No trick here. Simplest way is to note the dates for the corresponding highs and count the months. Repeat the process for the cyclical lows. If you know someone clever enough with Excel, the counting of the months can be done by the computer.

BRIAN SAYS

A distribution company that had nationwide sales asked us to look at its data to determine how it related to the leading indicators and specific markets. Early in our investigation, our client was amazed to learn that it was already in the weakening side of the business cycle (Phase C) and that its markets were deteriorating toward a recession in the next year. Our client had anticipated nothing but blue skies and strong sales for at least another two years. Since we were able to show our client where it was in the business cycle, it had time to be proactive and adjust to the changing market conditions. Our client was able to change its plans, make new arrangements, and not pour good money down the drain.

Start off listing each timing relationship through highs in one column and then through lows in another column. After simply jotting down the actual timing difference in months (noting who leads and who lags), rank the actual results for the highs, and then do it for the lows (you learned how to do this in Chapter 3).

When doing this, ABM found that it is normal for the company to lead the economy (as measured by US Industrial Production) through lows by three to nine months with a typical response time of four months.

MAKE YOUR MOVE>>> After you determine how the trends for your business compare to those in the general economy, complete the picture by using the same methodology to learn how your trends stack up with those in your industry. A comparison with your industry will enable you to determine how you are doing in relation to your peers. When you can make or acquire a credible 12/12 rate-of-change forecast of the trends in your industry, you can then estimate when your business will be transitioning through the upcoming phases of the business cycle based on the overall performance of the industry.

Besides determining the timing relationship between ABM Corp and the general economy (using US Industrial Production), we run the same process to find out how the company compares to the industry to which it belongs. Then take it to the next step and run the comparative analysis between the company and specific markets it serves. We are now compiling a wealth of information. What we know so far is presented in Illustration 5-4.

Illustration 5-4: What we know so far.

1. What is normal for the company to experience based on its own cycles
2. What forthcoming changes in the general economy mean to the company
3. How we are performing relative to our industry and what the industry forecast means for us
4. How we are relating to various markets and which markets are best for us to focus on and what the projected trend reversals in these markets mean for our company.

ALAN SAYS

Knowing information on rates-of-change can provide you with a gigantic competitive advantage. In addition to tracking the trends in your industry, follow the movement in industries that best represent your clients and customers. The rate-of-change information for their industries will show you the economic turns they will be facing. It will help you see what's ahead for them well before they become aware of the changes in store for themselves! Communicating this information to your clients and customers will strengthen your relationships with them and help you build long lasting partnerships.

ECO-SENSE

All your major markets may not move through the same business cycle at the same time. So, if you take the extra step of looking at *each of your major markets,* you can more effectively allocate your resources, which can be vital when your resources are limited. You can focus time, energy, and funds on rising markets while deemphasizing declining markets until they turn around.

Step Three – Calculate the timing relationship to key leading indicators

The third step in identifying where you are in the business cycle is to compare how you stack up to reliable, external leading indicators. As we've stated, leading indicators are a prime tool in determining when the business cycle will change for an industry or a company. However, before we begin our comparison, some points should be kept in mind:

A. The first leading indicators that go through a cyclical trend reversal may provide as much as a year's advanced warning that a shift in the industry or company cyclical trend is at hand. These shifts can be either upward or downward, depending on where you are in the business cycle. Financial leading indicators, which include bond prices, stock market prices, and the money supply, often provide the most lead time. For instance, the Corporate Bond Prices 12/12 established a low in November 2008. Its ascent was the first empirical sign we had that the recession of 2008-2009 would likely turn around and become the recovery of 2010.

B. Leading indicators reverse well in advance of the confirming indicators. Confirming indicators appear to shift direction almost simultaneously along with your own company. As we mentioned in Chapter 2, confirming indicators include changes in the temporary work force, decreased unemployment, and new orders for nondefense capital goods. Coincidental indicators are then followed by lagging indicators, which are as scattered and spread apart as the initial leading indicators. Lagging indicators include consumer expectations, unemployment statistics, sales force reports, and media news.

C. The manner in which the first few indicators rise or decline can provide a valuable insight into the dynamics of your future trend probabilities for the series that have yet to reverse direction. For instance, a sharp ascent in one or several of the leading indicators can be a signal that the rate of recovery for the ABM Corp will be correspondingly sharp.

D. Any leading indicator may move "out of synch" during a business cycle. For this reason, it is best to use a *system* of leading indicators in estimating your timing. Then use coincidental indicators that follow the earliest leading indicator turns to confirm or refute the earlier input.

You can use a myriad of leading indicators. To find what works for your business, start with the list we provided in Chapter 2; it probably includes all the leading indicators you will need.

The top seven leading indicators are

- Corporate Bond Prices 12/12 rate-of-change
- EcoTrends˙ Leading Indicator
- Purchasing Managers Index 1/12 rate-of-change
- US Leading Indicator 1/12 or 12/12 rate-of-change
- Orders vs. Inventory Levels
- Stock Market (S&P 500) 1/12 and 12/12 rates-of-change
- Housing Starts 12/12 rate-of-change.

These seven leading indicators should provide a ready source of information that will help you see around upcoming bends in the economy. Leading indicator information is also available for Canada, Europe, China, Mexico and many other countries.

Putting leading indicators to work

Construct visual 12/12 rate-of-change comparison charts using Excel or some other charting software. Your chart will reveal (1) the timing relationship between the series and (2) information about the future trend dynamics of the subject series based upon the earlier-turning indicators.

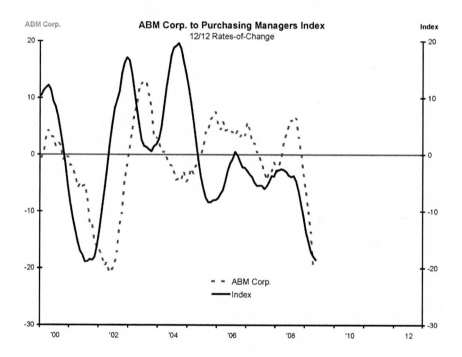

Chart 5-5: ABM Corp. to the Purchasing Managers Index

Notice that the shape of the trend in the Purchasing Managers Index tends to tell us something about what we can expect from the trend in the ABM Corp 12/12. Here is a trick for you. For either the 12/12 comparison or for data trend comparisons, substantially different series can be compared simply by scaling the company series on the left side of the chart and the leading indicator to the right side of the chart.

ECO-SENSE

Our research at the Institute for Trend Research tells us that we can learn more from leading indicators than just information about timing. We can also use leading indicator rate-of-change data to tell us how steep or how mild a future general economic trend is likely to be.

After the company data series and the leading indicator(s) have been charted, answer the following questions listed in Illustration 5-6.

Illustration 5-6: Leading indicator criteria questions.

1. Does one series consistently lead or lag the other series?
    a. If the answer is 'yes', we have found a leading indicator!
    b. If the answer is no, move on and try another indicator.
2. Does the timing relationship look fairly consistent?
    a. Consistency is good but not always possible to achieve.
    b. The more consistent the timing relationship the more faith you tend to put in what it is telling you is going to happen to the company.
3. Are the slopes of the rising/declining trends similar?
    a. Similarity is a wonderful thing because we are also getting some valuable input into how fast or how slow the trend is going to be for the company.
    b. Don't worry if the slopes are dissimilar; you still may have a useful leading indicator.
4. Are the series logically related?
    a. If 'yes', then this is a leading indicator that will be easy to use in management meetings and to convince other folks that change is coming.
    b. If 'no', then the leading indicator can still be useful but be prepared for people to chew up time trying to noodle out why this thing works. There usually is a logic stream, but it may not be obvious. The economy is a complicated symphony.

5. Is the series easily acquired and thus maintainable?
    a. There is no sense getting a leading indicator that is infrequently updated or otherwise available.
    b. Leading indicators should be checked once a month.
6. Are the series perhaps "counter-cyclical" with the rise in one being an indicator of decline in the other and vice versa?
    a. Sometimes this happens, and it isn't a bad thing. It usually means the company does well when this adverse condition (adverse to others anyway) is present, and we go down when other folks are happy.
    b. Counter-cyclical moves can be great indicators for businesses.

Chart 5-5 shows how a typical 12/12 comparison chart might look. Note that the chart meets the characteristics listed above with the exception of #6 (these series are not counter cyclical). Meeting the first five of our leading indicator criteria questions means we have found a useful road sign to the business.

After you have identified a useful leading indicator, do the following:

*   Determine the median and centered majority range timing relationships for the leading indicator to the company data series at both cyclical highs and lows. The mechanics will be no different than they were when you compared the timing relationships between the 3/12 and the 12/12 rates-of-change and compared US Industrial Production to our ABM Corp figures.
*   Count the number of months between related peaks
*   Rank the intervals between peaks
*   Determine the median and centered majority range timing relationships
*   Repeat the process for the business cycle lows

This is the ranking you created in Chapter 3. It must be repeated for each leading indicator you discover for the company.

ECO-SENSE

Complete the above process using as many leading indicators as you want or need. The more leading indicators you use, the more confident you can be. Start by using five of the seven that we listed. If they all agree, you usually can feel safe. However, don't forget that any single indicator can mislead you at a most inopportune time. So think about using more because a confluence of leading indicators will increase your chances of making the most correct timing conclusion.

At this point it might be useful to use another indicator such as the Corporate Bond Prices 12/12 in addition to the Purchasing Managers Index. With multiple indicators you get a fuller, richer picture and can make more pinpointed decisions.

The Corporate Bond Prices 12/12 will lead the ABM Corp 12/12 through a low by a median of 15 months. The Corporate Bond Prices 12/12 established a low in November 2008, which means that the ABM Corp 12/12 can be expected to pass through a low in February 2010 (median timing input). We can expect the company to transition from Phase D into Phase A in the first quarter of 2010.

ALAN SAYS

Let's stop for a minute and consider the full implication of what we have just done. You now have an accurate, reliable, external leading indicator that will give you a 15-month advance notice of when changing economic conditions will impact your company. But you still have work to do. Compare your results to other leading indicators. Fortunately, you have given yourself a year and a quarter to plan and prepare to execute actions that will keep your company profitable and ahead of the competition in terms of getting ready for the new business cycle rising trend. And you did it all while your competitors sat around wondering when (or if!) the economic downturn would ever end. While they are tentative and thinking in terms of "maybe" and "potential," you're being proactive —planning and getting ready to make your moves for the next recovery based on empirical input!

Illustration 5-7: What we now know so far.

1. What is normal for the company to experience based on its own cycles (from Step One)
2. What forthcoming changes in the general economy mean to the company (from Step Two)
3. How we are performing relative to our industry and what the industry forecast means for us (from Step Two)
4. How we are relating to various markets and which markets are best for us to focus on and what the projected trend reversals in these markets mean for our company (from Step Two)
5. What the aggregate timing input is from our system of leading indicators (Step Three)

Step Four – Complete the timing analysis table

For the final step, complete the Timing Analysis Table, shown below.

TIMING ANALYSIS TABLE **Determine When Your 12/12 Will Transition From Phase D into Phase A**			
Leading Indicator	**Low Date**	**No. of Mos**	**Timing Estimate**
Corporate Bond Prices 12/12	_____	_____	_____
EcoTrends® Leading Indicator	_____	_____	_____
Purchasing Managers Index 1/12	_____	_____	_____

US Leading Indicator 1/12	_____	_____	_____
Orders vs. Inventories	_____	_____	_____
Stock Prices 12/12	_____	_____	_____
Housing Starts 12/12	_____	_____	_____
US Industrial Production	_____	_____	_____
Normal 12/12 length of decline	_____	_____	_____
Input if a 3/12 low occurred	_____	_____	_____

Table 5-8: Blank Timing Analysis

Please note that Table 5-8 exactly as you see it will not be used when the leading indicators are approaching a business cycle high. However, a similar table can be constructed when you are forecasting when you are likely to transition from Phase B to Phase C and looking for the leading indicators and US Industrial Production to pass through highs.

You now have a complete data set from which to work. Rank the median cases you entered onto Table 5-8 to find the median timing input for when the company will establish a 12/12 business cycle low.

The estimated 12/12 low tells you that the 12MMT can be expected to reach at a low x number of months later. ABM Corp's 12/12 and 12MMT had a coincident timing relationship at lows, therefore, the timing for the 12/12 (for instance February 2010) would give us February 2010 for the 12MMT data trend low. You can now be confident that a transition from Phase D to Phase A will occur around February 2010 and a recovery awaits you. This would be the time to review Phase A Management Objectives™.

We occasionally use the majority range cases instead of the median timing inputs because the leading indicators' median timing estimates may not always align in a neat, tight range. In those cases, look at the centered majority range possibilities of the rogue cases to determine if the timing estimates you developed when you ranked the other cases fits into the centered majority range estimates of the rogues. For example, our median input is February 2010, but the US Leading Indicator component from the Table 5-8 may have had a median input of November 2010. Does the majority range input we calculated between the US Leading Indicator and the company allow for a February 2010 low? If it does, great! If not, keep in mind we have a rogue case that might be telling us something worthwhile, especially as we approach February, but go with the preponderance of the input from the system of leading indicators.

ABM Corp's management has completed all the hard work and now has to put it all together. When they do, they can be confident that ABM will not be surprised as they were in 2008. When you follow the same steps, you can also be confident that you will know when your recovery will begin.

ECO-SENSE

Although the recession of 2008-09 was dramatic and painful, it did not produce many declines that were longer than normal. Pay attention to what constitutes normal. When your estimates tell you that changes in trends will be either longer or shorter than normal, double check your calculations.

Remember

Forecasting with accuracy is now at your fingertips. Like many new learning experiences, it may take a little time for you to get the system in place. However, after you do it a few times, you will feel more comfortable and get the hang of it. When you do, you won't regret it. When you can successfully pinpoint what the economic pressures will be on your business a year from now, you will have a powerful competitive advantage that will catch your competitors completely off guard.

In our presentations, we often use the title, "The Future is Your Decision." Now you can see the future — and you can see it more clearly than you probably thought possible. Those insights will help you make the best decisions. We will be discussing those decisions in subsequent chapters.

WHAT TO DO NEXT

If you have not already done so, go to our website, www.ecotrends.org, use the Make Your Move button, and download the rate-of-change template and fill in your data. Follow the outline in this chapter and complete your own Timing Analysis Table. Before you start making decisions on where you want to be, learn where you are now and where you are going to be in the future. Then you can move ahead with more certainty and assurance.

TOP 10 RULES FOR MANAGING THE BUSINESS CYCLE

1. Realize that your business and that of your customers and clients are subject to the influences of cyclical change.

2. Develop objective means of measuring changes in your company's rate of growth.

3. Always know what phase of the business cycle your company is in and whether it is in the beginning, middle, or end of that phase.

4. Understand where each of your markets is in the business cycle and if it is leading or lagging.

5. Develop and learn how to use a system of leading indicators to project your company's future.

6. Develop a culture within your company that understands that change is a continual process and is dedicated to keeping your company evolving with your markets.

7. Ask yourself on a regular basis, "What don't I know?"

8. Find markets that are relatively acyclical or impacted to a less-than-average degree by business cycles.

9. Understand that your personnel will tend to resist change and that you must be prepared to lead with certainty and clarity.

10. Be willing to quickly adapt your business practices and procedures in accordance with changes in the business cycle and your markets.

CHAPTER 6
NOT-FOR-PROFIT ORGANIZATIONS

He who bestows his goods upon the poor, shall
have as much again, and ten times more.

John Bunyun

When people look at the economic landscape, not-for-profit organizations are often overlooked. However, that can be a mistake because not-for-profit companies are a force. In 2008, revenues for the 1.8 million IRS recognized tax-exempt organizations in the US reached $1.9 trillion dollars. That's a lot of revenue! These groups also employed about 6.6 million people.

The not-for-profit sector is a huge industry. It takes in about the same amount of money as is annually spent on new orders for durable consumer goods in the US. Another way to look at this behemoth is to realize that not-for-profit organizations, based on revenue, are larger than the six largest companies in the world combined, with about $73 billion to spare. By the way, $73 billion happens to be about the size of the US Postal Service.

Not-for-profit businesses are not *non-profit* entities. To survive, they must bring in more than they spend. Not-for-profits must be business-like and be well managed. They can't just bumble along and expect wealthy benefactors to continually bail them out.

Not-for-profits have tight budgets and their services are in great demand. Since every dollar counts, they can't afford to allocate their resources wastefully or inefficiently. So they are managed by skilled professionals. Like for-profit businesses, they need to forecast and carefully plan for the future.

Since so many not-for-profits act to ease human suffering, they must continually replenish their funding in order to carry out their missions. So their management and efficiency are critical — especially now that contributions are down and the need for their services has increased.

At the Institution for Trend Research, we've had the good fortune to work with many not-for-profit corporations and support their outstanding work. So we know first-hand the unique problems they face, the importance of forecasting for them, and the specific steps they must take.

Uniqueness of non-profits

Not-for-profit organizations come in a wide variety of sizes and shapes and they perform many different services. They focus on areas such as education, health care, research, disaster relief, religion, community service, public-aid, advocacy, and politics to name just a few. In size, they range from the largest —the Bill and Melinda Gates Foundation with an endowment of $35.1 billion — to family or individual foundations and scholarship funds, and everything in between.

In the US, we have about 350,000 religious not-for-profit organizations. In 2008 they took in $106.9 billion and 32.8% of those funds were personal charitable contributions.

From a business standpoint, not-for-profit groups face a number of unique challenges. They must efficiently provide effective services that require capital and capacity despite having the following difficulties:

- Unreliable and uneven funding. Since not-for-profits rely on the support of others, they may not receive funds, or they may receive fewer funds when their benefactors are suffering financially. In many cases, not-for-profits receive donations based on what their supports have left. For many benefactors, not-for-profits are at the bottom of the generosity chain.

- Volunteer, irregular, and transient staffing. Not-for-profits frequently rely on unpaid help who come and go (creating constant turnover) and work irregular hours or shifts. Therefore, they can often be understaffed. Not-for-profits must continually train new volunteers who can take longer to get up to speed because they work irregularly. Since they rely on unpaid help, not-for-profits may not be able to be too selective, so their staffs' efficiency may not be top notch.

- Paid staff members who work long hours for low pay. Although personnel may be devoted, they bear heavy loads that can wear them down and burn them out. Repeatedly working with those in need can be difficult, depressing and frustrating since there are no real products or services to sell, not-for-profits usually do not:

  A. Offer specials, promotions or rely on market penetration to offset slumping revenues. Although a symphony orchestra adds to the quality of people's lives, supporting it is not essential to their lives. In tough times, buying tickets and making contributions decline. So the fact that the symphony has a monopoly in a city is no hedge for it in a downturn because discretionary spending is one of the first things to go.

B. Bundle products or services. For-profit enterprises can offer a haircut for $70 and a manicure for $30 or charge $85 if you get them both today. Although our symphony may be able to bundle its ticket sales, other not-for- profits, including religious organizations, don't have that option.

C. Leverage product enhancements. For-profit businesses can bring in more revenue by enhancing their products, but most not-for-profits cannot. They may hope that enhanced services will help them raise funds, but it will usually only increase their traffic flow, leaving them faced with having to do more with the same amount of funds.

D. Reduce their costs. If not-for-profits reduce their costs, conditions will worsen in their communities. A real estate company can downsize from 14 to 7 people in tough times to weather economic storms. However, during similar downturns, a mental health facility may have to add personnel to meet increased needs. It might have to increase its staff from 14 to 21.

Since not-for-profit organizations have fewer options than for-profit groups, they have a greater need to accurately forecast upcoming economic trends and promptly respond to them. If they can't obtain the funding they need, their only option may be to cut costs. Not-for-profits hate to cut costs because it means that they will also have to decrease the vital services they provide to their communities.

Not-for-profit businesses must use every forecasting tool at their disposal to find out (1) where they are in the business cycle and (2) when their funds will increase or decrease. Only then can they effectively plan, manage, and chart their own course instead of being surprised by changes and then having to react to them.

Not-for-profits and the economy

According to Blackbaud's 2008 State of the Nonprofit Industry Survey, industry participants misread the outlook for 2009 because their forecasts were too optimistic. They also may have thought that the changing economy would not cause their revenues to drop.

Chart 6-1 below compares the Total Revenues 12/12 rate-of-change for not-for-profit organizations in the US and with the US Industrial Production 12/12 from 1996 into 2009. Chart 6-1 illustrates the cyclical identity. It shows that not-for-profits feel the decline in the economy and must adjust accordingly. They also benefit from upturns in economic activity and can use those periods to their long-term advantage.

We are proud to let you know that our publisher, Morgan James Publishing, will donate $1 to Habitat for Humanity for every copy of this book it sells. So buy a bunch. We each personally support other not-for-profit enterprises. Alan and his wife, Dawn, support CAM (Christian Aftercare Ministries for recently released prisoners) and His Mansion (an addiction rehabilitation center). Brian and his wife Joan support World Vision, The Smile Train, and Campus Crusade for Christ.

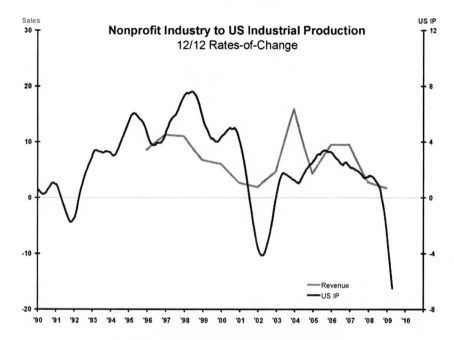

Chart 6-1. Rate-of-Change Comparison
for Not-for-Profit Industries

The fact that the a cyclical relationship exists between the rate-of-change for not-for-profit groups and US Industrial Production means that many not-for-profit organizations can utilize the same leading and coincidental indicators as their for-profit cousins. So using internal leading indicators, external leading indicators and accurately forecasting economic trends can enable not-for-profit organizations to manage their operations and fulfill their missions.

Did you notice that Chart 6-1 shows that unlike US Industrial Production, the Total Revenue 12/12 for not-for-profit organizations has not fallen below zero percent growth? Although their revenues may have slowed dramatically, growth in the not-for-profit industry has continued for the last 13 years. However, that rate of growth varies through time.

ECO-SENSE

When you compare the Total Revenue 12/12 rate-of-change for not-for-profits with the 12/12 rate-of-change for stock prices, something interesting appears. Take a look at Chart 6-2 below. Notice that the not-for-profit organizations' 12/12 *leads* the stock prices 12/12. The not-for-profit's revenues, which come from a myriad of sources, *anticipate* changes in the stock market!

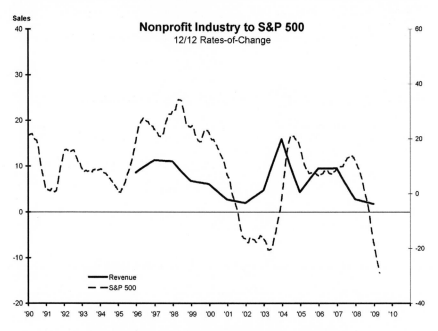

Chart 6-2. 12/12 Rate-of-Change for Not-for-Profits to Stock Market Prices

MAKE YOUR MOVE>>> Although you would not want to bet your entire portfolio on this observation, the relationship can be used by charitable organization administrators and by investors alike. When the stock market is falling, not-for-profits should watch out because things are going to get tougher for them. Conversely, when the stock market rices rise, management at those not-for-profit organizations can feel more secure that the increase in their revenues is probably not just a blip, but the beginning of sustained improvement in the income they will receive.

Similarly, if investors watch the trends in donations, it will give them a reasonable indicator of when they should move in and out of the stock market.

Since not all not-for-profits are created equally, you may be thinking, "Sure, it generally seems to make sense, but will it work for my organization? After all, mine differs from the aggregate."

Good question. Let's answer it by looking at different organizations of varying function and size. As we do, see how your group fits or whether it faces the same issues as any of the following not-for-profits. As you read about each of these groups, examine whether you could make its approach work for your business.

American Cancer Society

The American Cancer Society is the nationwide, community-based, voluntary health organization that is committed to eliminating cancer and diminishing suffering from cancer through research, education, advocacy, and service. The Society has 13 major divisions, over 2 million volunteers and over 3400 local offices nationwide. Revenue for 2008 for the combined operation was slightly over $1 billion. Any way you look at it, running the American Cancer Society is no easy task! Our present economy has not made that task any easier, despite the ever-present need and worthiness of the ACS's goals.

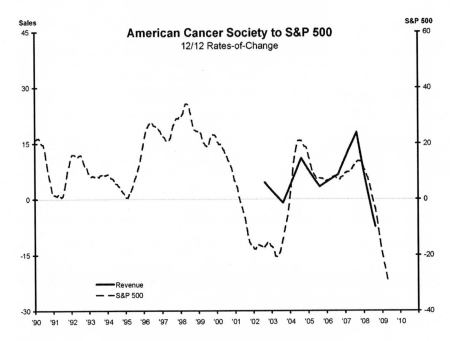

**Chart 6-3 American Cancer Society
Revenues Compared to Stock Prices**

Chart 6-3 shows how giving to the American Cancer Society (and other not-for-profit organizations) relates to trends in the stock market. This relationship affects whether contributions to the ACS rise or decline as well as the health of its endowments.

We know that changes in the stock market are a function of the economy in general. Now we also all know that the stock market tends to be a leading indicator to general economic changes in the US. Unfortunately, if the American Cancer Society waits for a recession to be generally recognized, it will be too late for it to make affective changes in its budgets and projected outlays. However, if it follows the leading indicators, tracks rates-of-change and carefully plans, it can prepare for and make the most of the future changes that will occur.

American Red Cross

The American Red Cross, founded in 1881 by Clara Barton, is perhaps the best-known emergency response organization in the world. Its mission is to offer neutral humanitarian care to the victims of war and help victims of natural disasters. Over the years, the American Red Cross has expanded its services to help needy community members, support members of the military and their families, provide lifesaving blood and blood products, promote educational programs on health and safety and conduct international relief and development programs.

ECO-SENSE

Endowments provide a major source of financial stability to many not-for-profit organizations. However, endowments are susceptible to swings in the business cycle. To protect themselves, not-for-profits should diversify their portfolios and consider placing funds in foreign investments to be less vulnerable to domestic shifts.

Much of the work that the American Red Cross provides is *event driven*, as opposed to the persistent needs that the American Cancer Society and other sharply-focused not-for-profits serve. Each year, victims of 70,000 disasters are helped by the American Red Cross. Since so much of the Red Cross' expenditures are made in response to specific major disasters, some might assume that the organization is impervious to changes in the economy. However, the opposite is true. Our research shows that the direction of the economy matters a great deal to the financial well being of the Red Cross.

According to its website, "An average of 91 cents of every dollar the Red Cross spends is invested in humanitarian services and programs. The Red Cross is not a government agency; it relies on donations of time, money, and blood to do its work." So knowing how it will fit into the economy is crucial to the American Red Cross.

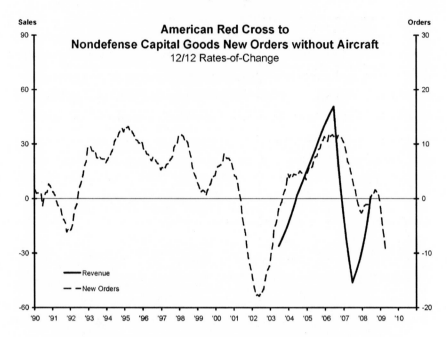

Chart 6-5. American Red Cross to Nondefense Orders

Chart 6-5 illustrates that American Red Cross Revenues are closely related to changes in Nondefense Capital Goods New Orders, which is an economic function and *not* the result of natural disasters.

Great causes – Whether the mission is to free the world of cancer or help disaster victims, it doesn't matter which, the economy is important to the fiscal well being of not-for-profit organizations and their ability to fund and carry out their missions. Like for-profit businesses, if they can foresee future economic trends, they can position themselves to make the most of them.

BRIAN SAYS

Wouldn't it be great if revenues for charitable organizations were counter-cyclical? If revenues went up when the economy went down? If that's how it worked, the supply of funds would rise when the need was greatest.

Our work shows that this isn't generally the case, but we as individuals can make a huge difference. Studies show that the types of folks likely to read this book are amongst the most giving folks around.

MAKE YOUR MOVE>>> When times are tough, try to give even more, especially to those who can't help themselves. Entrepreneurs and business leaders should take the lead because they have the power to change the world in so many different and positive ways!

Mental Health Center of Denver

Now, let's look at a local organization that performs outstanding community services. The Mental Health Center of Denver, CO is a private, charitable organization that annually serves 11,500 people (adults and children). It employs more than 500 professionals in its seven outpatient clinics, 23 residences, and three homeless shelters. Everyday the Center takes one homeless person off the street.

We have included the Mental Health Center of Denver in our discussion of not-for-profit groups because its scope of operation is limited to one local area. We want to make sure that our examination does not look just at big national or international organizations. Understanding the national economy can be of great help to city-sized organizations as well as larger not-for-profits.

Funding and efficiency are critical for the Mental Health Center of Denver, as it is for similar operations throughout the country. Revenue limitations and the misalignment of resources can cause ongoing, untreated health problems which can severely affect the local workforce, you, and your neighbors.

Before you get depressed, good news also exists. The Mental Health Center of Denver has a cyclical relationship to the US economy (see Chart 6-6 below). The Industrial Production 12/12 typically leads the Center through highs by 12 months and through lows by 7 months (median timing). A projected October 2009 US Industrial Production 12/12 low implies that the Center will pass through a low in May 2010.

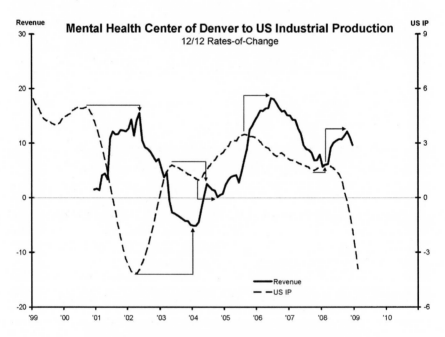

Chart 6-6. Mental Health Center of Denver to US Industrial Production

> ### ECO-SENSE
>
> By using the leading indicators presented in this book, the Mental Health Center of Denver has had at least one years' advance notice of upcoming business cycle changes. This gave the center's CEO, Carl Clark, M.D., and his team plenty of time to find alternative sources of funding and prepare for slower growth. The Center was able to plan and stay true to its mission of helping people because Dr. Clark was able to see around the next curve and make the appropriate adjustments.

Lancaster (PA) Symphony Orchestra

Using a symphony orchestra as an example seems especially appropriate given our belief that economics and music have so much in common. This example can also switch gears by moving our discussion of not-for-profit organizations from health care and disaster relief to the arts.

Mr. Rick Oppenheimer is the Chairman of the Board of this $1.7 million dollar organization. He is justifiably proud of the orchestra's accomplishments and credits its success to its "exceptionally talented musicians and music director (Maestro Stephen Gunzenhauser)." Less than 50% of the orchestra's funding comes from ticket sales and the balance is received through charitable contributions, sponsorship of particular events and sources such as the National Endowment for the Arts.

When the Lancaster Symphony Orchestra debuted on May 01, 1947, ticket prices ranged from $1.20 to $2.40. The profit from its initial concert totaled $236. Ironically, the City of Lancaster, PA had wanted to start an orchestra earlier, but was prevented from doing so by two world wars and the depression of the '30s.

According to Mr. Oppenheimer, the 2008-09 recession has left the symphony "struggling." Contributions are "definitely going down and it is hard to get people to be supportive," given the current economic climate. An income deficit has developed because symphony productions have high artistic appeal, but do not generate enough revenue to cover their costs. Although some would like to continue this process and wait it out, the economy will probably force a change.

The orchestra will have to adjust to lower revenues. Oppenheimer believes that means designing programs that will fit smaller budgets and focusing on "Mr. Everyday so more people will come." Costs must also be cut. Over the last eight years, which was a time of great prosperity in the country and the region, the symphony added eight people. "Now," Oppenheimer said, "It's time to cut staff and adjust to reality.

> The decisions faced by not-for-profit organizations differ only slightly from those faced by profit-making businesses. In the not-for-profit world, the term "profits" is replaced by "surplus," but the need to generate surpluses that can be retained and reinvested is equally crucial. Knowing how the economy is going to perform will help both insure that their profits and surpluses will continue.

Religious Not-for-Profit Organizations

Giving to religious organizations went *up* 5.5% in 2008 from 2007 — even though the economy was tanking! Over the years, we have observed that most business leaders, CEOs, and entrepreneurs really enjoy "giving back" in one form or another.

A 5.5% increase in personal charitable contributions to religious organizations tells us that Americans are a giving people with a strong penchant for helping their fellow man. To get a fuller perspective, look at the following figures. They show how a 5.5% gain stacks up with the amounts Americans spent for other items in 2008. They are:

- Groceries   +5.5%
- Full-service restaurants   +2.2%
- Sporting goods   +0.1%
- Retail jewelry sales   -8.1%
- Total retail sales   +1.0%

This data proves the following:

1. We view giving as an extremely important part of our lives,
2. While we are willing to cut in many areas, religious contributions are slow to feel a downturn.

Having said that, understand that religious giving is not impervious to economic assault. Religious charitable giving is likely to go down in 2009 as more and more people are confronted by the harsh economic reality of the recession. Administrators of not-for-profit organizations must look to increased efficiencies and cash-saving initiatives in tough times.

ALAN SAYS

From my personal experience with several organizations, I've observed that the members' commitment to the group and its goals are driving forces that keep contributions at the level necessary to maintain the organizations' objectives. To stay on track and continue fulfilling your mission, clearly explain to your supporters what you are trying to accomplish. If you clarify the problems and state how you plan to handle them, you will demonstrate good stewardship and engender supporters' trust.

MAKE YOUR MOVE>>> Keep your supporters informed and hold expenditures down. Transparency in reporting and flat salaries will go a long way in keeping budgets sound and making givers happy and supportive.

Remember

Think of all the good work that cannot be accomplished when turns in the economy catch not-for-profit organizations by surprise. The fact that not-for-profits have lofty and laudable missions and special tax status does not excuse them from following good business practices. The winds of change don't have a moral compass; they can strike everyone, everywhere.

To fulfill their missions most efficiently, get the most out of every dollar and maximize the effectiveness of their operations, every not-for-profit must learn to determine what economic conditions it will face. It must learn how to forecast and determine what lies in store so it can plan, prepare and make the right moves. Millions of needy people will be counting on it.

CHAPTER 7
MANAGEMENT OBJECTIVES™ FOR PHASE A

Some single mind must be master, else there
will be no agreement on anything.
Abraham Lincoln

The scene is played out about 200 times a year. It doesn't matter whether we're speaking to 15 executives at a Vistage International® meeting or 400 business leaders at the Grand Rapids Economic Club. Before we begin, we always have the same two concerns:

- Will they believe us?
- Can we help them be more successful?

The answers are a resounding yes and yes!

As to question 1, our audience will believe us because we can give them empirical leading indicators that they will understand and trust. However, question 2 is much more personal. While we definitely can show them how to make timely application of our Management Objectives™, an elephant is in the room: will the leaders we address act in time?

As we've pointed out, the business cycle consists of four phases. In this chapter, we will discuss the first, Phase A.

In Phase A, the business cycle is advancing. The economy's momentum is on the upswing, and data that showed that it had been in recession is starting to turn in a positive direction. This is the phase of the cycle that everyone is looking for as we write this book. Phase A is illustrated by Chart 7-1.

To spot this change and be confident that the business cycle is actually improving, companies can rely on two historically verifiable measures. These measures signal that an upward trend is taking place:

(1) The majority of the leading indicators that the company depends upon are moving up.
(2) The company's 12/12 rate-of-change, which measures the business' growth for 12 consecutive months, is rising.

Phase A

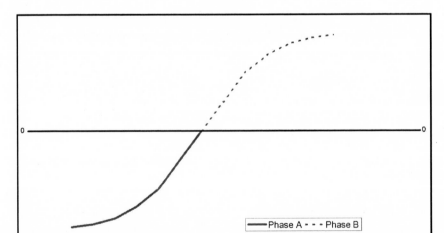

Chart 7-1. 12/12 rate-of-change is rising toward the zero.

MAKE YOUR MOVE >>> When both of these signs are present, be confident that the economy is moving into the better part of the business cycle. Then act! Start planning the specific steps you will take to capitalize the upturn.

Confirm your decision to act by comparing the signaling measures with your company's 3/12 rate-of-change. The 3/12 rate-of-change is based on data for a consecutive 3-month period during one calendar year, while the 12/12 rate-of-change uses the data for 12 consecutive months. When the 3/12 rate-of-change rises above the 12/12 rate, it confirms that the momentum for the cycle for your company is actually shifting. The same holds true when the 3/12 dips below the 12/12, which tells you that the cycle is losing momentum.

Conflicting messages

Early Phase A can be a confusing time. Although the economy shows encouraging signs, most decision makers are still pessimistic, fearful, and uncertain. Since the economy has been in the dumps, an overall sense of gloom still prevails. Most of the news, analysis, and scuttlebutt remain negative, and no one is sure when the economy will improve. At this time, even optimists become guarded and the old adage, "It's always darkest before the dawn" seems to have been coined for these times.

To determine when a trend has started and when it will end, we use a number of specific quantitative means in our work at ITR®. The good news is that you don't have to go into the same detail. If your 12/12 rate-of-change rises for three or more months and your 3/12 climbs above your 12/12 rate-of-change, a viable cyclical rising trend is in progress. The downside also applies. However, since we're concentrating on preparing for better days, let's focus on the upside.

To request more information on these turning points, go to our website, www.ecotrends.org, or simply call us at 603.796.2500 and ask one of our analysts.

When business leaders see the signs that the business cycle may be advancing toward recovery, many are afraid to act because the world around them is still so pessimistic. The idea of taking aggressive action goes against their instincts and seems out of step with everyone else. When these executives look at the instruments on the dashboard — the leading indicators and 12/12 rate-of-change — they see optimistic signs, but when they gaze out the window, they see something else —the dense fog of doom and gloom. As a result, leadership can be reluctant to move forward at this time.

<u>ALAN SAYS</u>

Leadership's reluctance was brought sharply into focus in April 2009. I was happy to receive an invitation to address a trade association in Orlando, Florida. Since the mood in the country was terrible, my task was clear — don't depress them any more than they already are. Instead, help them look forward and focus more on what is coming, which fortunately involved some good news.

Mistakenly, I assumed that my task would be simple. My plan was to spend a good part of the hour discussing the two leading indicators that had already turned positive, another one that was hinting at moving that way, and then address the remaining leading indicators. To set a positive tone, I pointed out how we Americans change, the danger of straight-line thinking and the risks involved in the prevalent pessimism. Then I outlined the clear action items that business leaders needed to take to prepare for the recovery.

Despite all the favorable information, the audience sat mired in gloom. Every question from the floor had the same defeatist worried theme, and only a few people in the audience were willing to look beyond today and see the opportunities in store. I left with a deep sense of disappointment knowing that in the years to come, a few of them would excel, but most of the others would settle for average returns.

The big question for decision makers is whether to believe the signs that the economy will be improving and therefore start to plan for the boom. Many won't move quickly because they're afraid that the signs may be wrong. Instead, they will "play it safe" and not go out on a limb. Like most of the business world, they will stand pat.

BRIAN SAYS

In Phase A, leadership and courage are crucial. This is when your leadership will be tested. Make prompt decisions; you can't afford to wait. Moving quickly can be hard. It may go against your instincts and against conventional wisdom, but it will separate you from the pack.

It takes great courage to take the lead, to step forward while everyone else is holding back. It's risky to exchange the comfort and safety of the group for the exposure of standing alone. When you move out of the pack, you can become an easy target. However, *risk taking and having courage are inherent in leadership.*

As companies advance further in Phase A, the mood changes internally from uncertainty to hope. A more positive and hopeful atmosphere slowly and guardedly emerges. More people feel that life will get better and the economy will improve. Soon it becomes generally accepted that the recovery is at hand. At that point, companies' competitors begin to make plans so they can cash in on the good times that everyone agrees are in store.

Don't delay

If you act early in Phase A and track your leading indicators and your company's 12/12 rate-of-change, you will have at least a six-month jump on your competition. By the time your competitors finally act and start to plan, you will be far ahead because your plans will be in place and you will have already started implementing them.

Don't wait until you are in Phase A to position yourself to take advantage of the upturn. If you do, it will be too late. Instead, watch the signals to see when Phase A is coming, gather your resources and plan. Then, when Phase A actually comes, you will have made your plans for the upswing and will know exactly what to do. At that point, all you have to do is implement those plans.

As much as you may want to see signs that good times are coming, they can be counterintuitive and hard to believe. Intellectually you may trust the statistics and know that they're correct, but emotionally you're still not able to climb fully on board.

At this point, act on the basis of the statistics, not on your guts. Believe the signs and take the risks. Since the signs are giving you information about the future that others haven't seen, they may make you doubt and feel out of synch. Accept that it can be difficult to see what will be happening in your business before others see it in their businesses.

MAKE YOUR MOVE >>> As you move into Phase A, change your thinking about money. Instead of hoarding cash, start to spend. Purchase new equipment for new markets, for cost efficiencies and for expansion into new areas. Buy your competitors. Think about borrowing money to leverage the rising trend.

In early 2009, DW Distribution Inc. of Dallas, TX hosted a conference for distributors of housing related products. Although the last year had been anything but kind, the mood at the conference was upbeat, not doom and gloom. The folks at DW Distribution had flat out refused to participate in

During the backside of the business cycle, chief financial officers or comptrollers are sage advisors; so listen to them. Invariably, they will tell you to conserve, cut spending, and build cash. However, when you see an upward trend and start getting ready for Phase A, listen to different voices — your sales and marketing people.

the recession. Everyone was eager to talk about 2010 and the actions they would take in anticipation of a slightly better year. As they planned for the future and made decisions based on a yet-unrealized recovery, their positive attitude was infectious. Their spirit may have reflected the true grit and independence of Texans, and if so, we could all stand to be a little more Texan.

As you move into Phase A:

- *Be entrepreneurial.* Entrepreneurs work smartly and creatively. They also work hard and don't let others tell them what they can't do. They set goals and reach them.

- *Move quickly and decisively.* Since Phase A is a time of change, opportunity and growth, take a "can do" attitude. Even though the market is soft, find ways to use its sluggishness to your advantage.

- *Don't be self-limiting.* Look for opportunities and don't say, "That's not our market." Instead, ask, "How can I get into that market?" Don't state, "We don't have the right person. Instead, declare, "Let's go out and get the right person."

Phase A Management Objectives ™

As the economy advances toward recovery, capitalize on the upswing by implementing the steps below that apply to your business:

Costs and savings

1. *Negotiate union contracts.* Since the workforce has recently experienced wide layoffs, labor leaders will be less concerned about the future than they are about the here and now. They usually won't push you as hard for raises and benefits because they're glad that their people have jobs. Phase A presents a golden opportunity for businesses to negotiate labor contracts because they can lock in lower labor costs for the next few years.

2. *Enter into leases.* Negotiate or renegotiate long-term leases on your fleet, machinery and, especially, real estate. Landlords and property managers cringe when we make this recommendation, but they know it makes sense. Due to the recent downturn, landlords are now concerned about their vacancy rates; so many will be willing to enter into win-win leases with potential or existing tenants. Landlords may make concessions on the rent and help tenants reduce their immediate cash flow needs in exchange for longer-term leases or pay backs at the end of lease terms. They may be more creative, especially in accepting deferrals to help their tenants survive.

3. *Know your break-even point.* Be keenly aware of your break-even point down to the last penny. Review it regularly because it will impact your pricing, budgets, expectations and profits. Know the sales levels you need to be profitable given your current cost structures because those amounts change over time. When businesses go through a trough, their break-even points may be lower than they were when they went into the decline. So the margins they must earn on each of their products and services and as a company will differ from what they were.

4. *Lock in commodity prices.* Generally, commodity prices are a lagging economic indicator. So as your business picks up and your future starts looking brighter, enter into long-term raw material contracts before the prices escalate. Making this commitment will take courage, but down the road, the fact that you locked in long-term supply contracts at today's low prices will save you a bundle.

Build the foundation for recovery

5. *Make acquisitions.* Use the prevailing pessimism to your advantage. In a downturn, the mood is gloomy. Business owners are tired and discouraged from trying to keep the business afloat

— especially when their profits are down and they are short on cash. They may have a fundamentally healthy business, but a fundamentally bad attitude and, therefore, question whether their efforts or their company is worth the uphill battle they face. If you make them an offer, they just may accept, and you can make a fabulous deal.

ECO-SENSE

As companies go through business cycle phases, their thinking changes. For example, those that once spent lavishly will tighten their belts, while firms that aggressively tried to enter new fields, will stop looking and focus exclusively on their core businesses. As phases of the cycle change, many of these businesses continue to follow policies tied to the previous phase of the business cycle, which can be a big mistake.

For instance, many companies keep their prices too low for too long in Phase A. As they implement our Phase A Management Objectives™, their cost structures rise. However, most do not raise their prices or raise them quickly enough — especially those that lowered them during the slump in order to hold onto their customers. After they lowered their prices, they became comfortable with them and don't want to risk losing business by raising them.

6. *Make capital expenditures and acquisitions.* Examine the potential of every opportunity. Base your decisions on longer-trend possibilities. Don't spend money trying to be the nation's largest paper manufacturer because it's a dying industry. Every opportunity differs; so don't expect each of them to grow evenly and make money. Instead, focus sharply and discriminate. Investigate lucrative new markets that you could enter and then go after them. Identify the long-term trends and how you can develop expertise consistent with those trends.

"The best opportunities are available if you have a strong cash position in Phase A," Bill Stockwell of Stockwell Elastomerics, Inc., points out. "We capitalized on the rapid recovery in the US Manufacturing sector in late 2003 and early 2004 by setting strategic deals with vendors and having a strong cash position. Despite our strong revenues, we've played things conservatively for the past six months while we waited for the 2009 event. In running a small manufacturing business, cash is king — and we have learned the banking community can be capricious in this phase of the cycle."

7. *Judiciously expand credit.* After a downturn, businesses tend to be gun shy in extending credit because they've been burned. Start loosening the reins. Recognize that the pendulum has swung and don't lose business because you're afraid to repeat the bad experiences of the last few years. Extend more credit to more customers, but don't go hog wild. Evaluate each case individually. Give more liberal terms to customers who deserve them and assume that more of your customers deserve to get better terms.

8. *Exploit your competitive advantages.* Find out what differentiates you and makes you better and more desirable to customers than your competitors. Don't just go on what you think. Hire firms that provide this information or interview your customers and vendors. Get specifics. If they say that you have a great service department, ask them why. Do you have more trucks, faster response time or solve problems 97% of the time on the first visit? When you identify your advantage, sharpen and accentuate it. Then vigorously promote that strength. If you don't have a competitive advantage, create one and exploit it.

For a great book on how to distinguish your business, we highly recommend *Creating Competitive Advantage*, by Jaynie L. Smith and William G. Flanagan (Broadway Business, 2006).

> ## *ECO-SENSE*
>
> Knowing your specific competitive advantages is vital because you may want to promote different advantages at different phases of the business cycle. On the down side, you probably want to tell your customers how you will save them money and help them sell to their accounts. On the up side, you usually want to stress your speed, reliability, efficiency, technical advances and excellence.

9. *Invest in customer market research.* Learn the precise goods and services your customers value, what they need, the prices they will pay and delivery terms they require. Find out why other businesses are not buying from you and what it would take for them to become your customers.

10. *Implement training programs.* Since business is on the ascent, it's vital that you have enough trained employees available when demand hits its peak. Anticipate how many orders will stream in and how many well-trained people you will need to handle them. Then hire and train them so you will be ready for the rush. If you don't, your customer service will suffer, you will alienate customers, and they may turn to other

Phase A is a period of change. Decide where to place your major emphasis, which risks to take, and where to spend money, time and energy. Before you make your final decisions and firm up your plans, it can help to speak with your vendors.

Vendors are outstanding sources of market intelligence. They know the trends and direction in which the industry is moving. Vendors can tell you which companies are buying, what they're buying, in what amounts and why. They know all the players, their financial positions and stability. As for personnel, vendors also know the top people, whether they are happy with their employers and would be a good fit with you, whether they would be willing to move and how much they would want.

sources. If customers leave because of poor or lack of service, it's murder to get them back.

People and leadership

12. *Lead with optimism and a "can do" attitude.* Early in Phase A, your employees will be scared, need reassurance and strong leadership. Show them that you have a plan and that you are confident that the company will succeed. If not, your staff could become demoralized and their productivity might drop. If your personnel are glum, it will be communicated to your customers. This vicious cycle starts when leadership shows weakness, and it can destroy your business. To avoid this problem, do more than just trying to motivate the troops; give them empirical reasons to be confident. Show them facts and figures: improved leading indicators and the company's rate-of-change.

13. *Provide positive leadership.* Be optimistic and energetic because your attitude will flow through your organization. Inspire, take a can-do attitude, set metrics, and determine goals because personnel throughout your organizations will follow your lead. Delegate authority and let others in your organization delegate their authority. Provide open atmospheres to foster creativity and growth. Accept that people make mistakes and don't react harshly. When people are punished for making mistakes, they won't take chances, which will limit your company's ability to grow in the next phase of the cycle, Phase B.

An excellent and enjoyable book on leadership and attitude is *Failing Forward: Turning Mistakes Into Stepping Stones For Success*, by John Maxwell (Thomas Nelson, 2007). It tells the stories of a number of business leaders who rebounded from setbacks to achieve success.

14. *Establish goals.* Set precise tactical goals that will bring about strategic achievements. Identify and define the steps that will

enable your people to carry out the company's strategies. All goals and destinations must be unmistakable and all plans detailed, ordered, and exact. It's one thing to say that you want to climb the mountain, but it's another to check out the site, assemble the crew, plan the route, buy the gear and hire the guide.

15. *Develop a measurement and accountability system.* Before you try to climb that mountain, decide what gear is needed, who will buy it, who will be hired as the guide, and who will buy what plane tickets. It's up to the leader to put people in positions of responsibility and make sure that they're accountable for achieving all goals. Leaders also must hold themselves accountable for seeing that the system they built is being followed and is working. If it's not, they must make all necessary adjustments.

16. *Hire top people.* During economic slumps, good people lose their jobs. In Phase A, lots of good people will still be out of work, or they will be working for companies that have no vision, strategy, and direction or are on the ropes. Many of these people will be looking for other employment opportunities. Since many top workers are available in Phase A, it's an ideal time to hire. If you wait until Phase B (the really good times), those people will probably be gone.

17. Align your compensation plans to be consistent with the metrics you establish for meeting your short-term tactical goals. Reward for performance not existence. For example,

    a. If your strategic vision is to have your annual revenue reach $20 million in three years, set firm goals and compensate your employees for reaching those goals.

    b. If your plan calls for you to have sales of $15 million the first year, then compensate your employees when they reach that plateau.

c. If your target for the following year is $18 million in sales, celebrate that achievement when it's reached.

Sometimes leading means being willing to go places that others don't. 2002 was a difficult year in the energy market and energy stocks were low. After Brian told Peter Boyd, CEO, President and Co-Founder of Arcis Corp., "Borrow as much money as you can because the cost is really cheap," Peter decided to replace Arcis' equity with debt. He also decided to take the company private, even though he previously had taken it public. Peter and his management team secured leverage buyout capital at an average of 8% while the cost of Arcis' equity was about 30%. They purchased the company for $25 million, but borrowed $24 million. That $1 million in equity produced $35 million in EBIDA in 2008.

"The interest rate was the most important part of the decision," Peter said. "I don't know if I would have had the courage to do this without a strong belief in ITR''s work.

Growth and expansion

18. *Develop and begin advertising and marketing programs.* In Phase A, you have more cash available to spend on advertising and marketing. You've also learned what your competitive advantages are and what your customers' value; so you should create a plan that will pound away on those points in order to attract more business. Your instinct may be to wait until the upswing is at full speed, but by then it could too late. Get a jump on the competition. Position yourself so that when businesses in your market start to recover, they will instantly think of you and recognize that you can immediately deliver what they need. Make your pipeline wide and short.

19. *Look for additional vendors.* The companies that supply your business are also hungry because they have gone through

difficult times. So they will be more willing to give you good deals. Having a number of vendors can be important because you don't want any one or two of them to be able to create a bottleneck in your pipeline.

Over the years, a client of ours had a consistently strong track record. Then, while the economy was doing well, our client's sales suddenly crashed. When we asked what happened, we were told that the vendor's factory burned. Our client had just one source and when that source couldn't deliver, our client went through a rocky period when its revenue virtually disappeared.

BRIAN SAYS

The new mantra is *China + 1 + 1*. If you're sourcing from China, your supplies could abruptly stop. Production can cease due to all sorts of reasons that may be completely beyond your control and getting back in gear may be hard or take forever. So play it safe: in addition to China, source from two other places so you have backups if your Chinese pipeline stops.

---

20. *Check that distribution systems can accommodate increased activity.* Make sure that your distribution network can handle the increased load that will build during Phase A. See to it that all parts of your operation are up to the task and that you have back ups to avoid bottlenecks. If you've been doing business with X Corp. for years and you're getting ready to grow in Phase B, be hardnosed. Realistically assess whether X Corp. can handle the increased load and look into other options.

21. *Invest in technology and software to improve your efficiency.* Keep in mind that as the business cycle ascends, the cost of technology will be a lot less than the cost of hiring more people. Investing in technology today will also be less expensive than

it will be a year or two from now. If you can supplant people with technology, do so!

22. *Implement your plans to expand facilities.* Don't wait until you're out of capacity before you decide to increase it. Too many companies wait until they are at the top of the business cycle to add capacity, but by the time that capacity comes on line, they don't need it any more. If you follow the leading indicators and your company's rate-of-change, you will be able to project upcoming economic trends and know which markets will be profitable in the coming years. Then make sure that you will have the capacity you'll need to fully serve those markets in 24 months. In addition, during Phase A, construction costs will be down, contractors will have shaved their margins and will be willing to work for a lot less.

23. *Add sales staff.* Most companies wait until Phase B to hire and train new sales people, which is usually too late. Companies tell us that it takes 9 to 12 months to train new sales personnel. Since Phase A lasts about 12 months, businesses should be hiring and training new sales people at the bottom of Phase A so when they move into Phase B, they are good to go. Put on enough people to handle the increased loads you project — don't be caught short. Have your sales force knock on doors that your company never approached before. The world will have changed since the last time you were gearing up for Phase B so don't assume that you will have the same markets and customers.

24. *Build inventories in your high-volume lines.* Have your inventories well stocked so you can promptly fill all the orders that will be streaming in. In your planning, consider how much lead-time you will need and what your turn rate will be when business improves. We know many companies that have increased their market share during the upside of the business cycle simply because they were prepared. When the good times returned,

they had merchandise on hand, but their competitors did not because they were still living in the recession.

25. *Place capital equipment orders.* Buying capital equipment in Phase A will be far cheaper than it will be later in Phase B. In Phase A, a great deal of both new and used equipment will be available at attractive prices and you will have more choices as to what you can buy. The lead-times will also be shorter at this phase of the business cycle than they will be down the road.

Downturns provide great opportunities for those who work with capital equipment. One of our clients bought a used machine from a company that was going out of business. He paid only $40,000 for a piece of equipment that was worth $200,000. Although our client had no immediate need for that machine, he recognized that he could use it at some future time. Sure enough, when his business picked up in Phase B, our client had that machine up and running and it helped him make lots of money.

26. *Begin phasing out low margin work.* When business is slow, most businesses will take on whatever work brings in cash. Frequently, that work doesn't contribute much to the bottom line, but it keeps the lights on and the workforce busy. However, when business improves, working for those low margins may no longer make sense. When the signs tell you that better days lie ahead, phase out low margin work to make way for business that will strengthen your bottom line. Focus on increasing your profits instead of just keeping cash in the pipeline.

Remember

In Phase A, the leading indicators forecast that the business cycle is moving toward better times, but decision makers are usually reluctant to trust them and are slow to move out of their recession thinking.

Essentially, they're afraid to make the wrong moves. At this point, leadership and courage are crucial. Leaders must act quickly to beat their competitors and position their companies for the flood of new business that will soon come.

Phase A is a period of change. It should be a building process and the main objective should be to position your company to make the most of the strong business atmosphere that will follow in Phase B. When you successfully prepare your company in Phase A, it will soar higher and farther in Phase B. In Phase A, leadership can change the slope of the curve and lengthen the rise beyond what your industry and competitors will experience. When all your plans are made, decisions are reached and actions are underway, you will be ready for Phase B, the best and busiest part of the business cycle.

TOP 10 MAJOR BUSINESS MISTAKES TO AVOID

1. Don't get your "view of the future" only from mass media outlets.

2. Don't assume that changes in the overall economy will not affect your business.

3. Don't assume that your business as it stands today is what it will need to be in the future.

4. Don't assume that you can afford to lose the entrepreneurial spirit as you move forward in your endeavors.

5. Don't compensate your employees by any other metric than their measurable performance.

6. Don't rely on just one or two leading indicators when you try to forecast the future.

7. Don't assume the future will repeat the past that you have known.

8. Don't be afraid to raise your prices when you have a true competitive advantage.

9. Don't assume that government intervention in the marketplace will not have unintended consequences

10. Don't forget to **MAKE YOUR MOVE >>>** when the time is right.

CHAPTER 8
MANAGEMENT OBJECTIVES™ FOR PHASE B

Not the cry, but the flight of the wild duck, leads the flock to fly and follow.
Chinese proverb

We're at beautiful Lake Geneva, WI waiting for ABM Corp.'s strategic planning meeting to start. The setting is idyllic and the mood is more relaxed than anyone has seen in years. A strong sense of pride and satisfaction fill the air. It's what you feel when you successfully steer your boat to safety after battling a violent summer storm. Everyone is upbeat and enthusiastic because sales have soared well over those of a year ago. You're ready to sail forth, expand your horizons and conquer new worlds.

Congratulations! – You're in Phase B, the Best part of the business cycle.

Phase B is a critical period. What you do in Phase B will affect your workplace for the entire business cycle. It will impact how many people keep their jobs when the economy eventually swings back around to Phase D, as well as the future course of the business, expansion plans, the framework for profitability and more. The responsibility is enormous.

Phase B defined

As you recall, Phase B is when your 12/12 rate-of-change is ascending above the 0 line (see Chart 8-1). Sales are running progressively higher than they did this time last year and revenues are climbing to the steepest portion of the rising trend.

Phase B

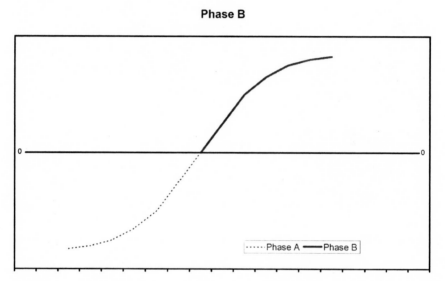

Chart 8-1: Phase B

Chart 8-1 shows Phase B of the business cycle when the 12/12 rate-of-change is rising higher and higher away from zero.

In many ways, Phase B is the best portion of the business cycle. It's usually the most exciting and exhilarating time. When you get up in the morning, you're raring to get to work because everything is fun, alive and captivating. Although managing this growth could create added stress in the latter half of Phase B, it's exciting to see the business grow and enjoy such success.

Amidst this euphoria, it's crucial to stay focused because seemingly innocuous decisions can have long-lasting and dangerous consequences.

The longer you are in Phase B and the higher your rate-of-change climbs, the more the potential dangers increase. However, these problems are manageable if you pay careful attention to the Management Objectives™ that we are about to explain.

ECO-SENSE

Inadequate planning in the latter stages of Phase D or slow execution in Phase A can lead to a host of "positive problems" in Phase B. Positive problems occur when too much business comes in the door and you have insufficient resources to reasonably manage it. When you have positive problems, your customers will become disgruntled because:

a) Their deliveries are late

b) Your office systems can't keep up with the load

c) Your quality slides in a "hurry to get it done" atmosphere

Disgruntled customers are the kiss of death. When your clientele are unhappy, your profits will drop and your market share will erode. Once you lose customers, getting them back is never easy. Avoid these pitfalls by being prepared and having enough of each of the factors of production to meet your forecasted needs in Phase B.

During Phase B, optimism reigns supreme. It's easy to get excited about how well the company is doing and to feel great about the future. Cash flow is good and most days fly by in a blur of positive activity. Everyone loves making money.

When you ask most people how long these good times will last, they optimistically say, "At least another six months." Although you know they can't last forever, you're confident that the bonanza will continue for at least another six months regardless of how long you have already been in Phase B.

So you push forward. You plan, expand, spend and acquire. You remain excited, energetic and dedicated to making the most of this fabulous time. However, in your enthusiasm, in your zeal, you can step off the curb into oncoming traffic because you didn't pay attention to the signal at the crosswalk that was brightly beaming red.

Regardless of how good you feel during Phase B, continue to look both ways and follow the signals before venturing out. To prolong the time you spend in Phase B and continue enjoying the momentum, productivity, and profits, follow our Phase B Management Objectives™, which are outlined below.

Phase B Management Objectives™

Our Phase B Management Objectives™ will help propel your business higher. They will show you how to hold onto your gains and avoid the common mistakes that occur as you move to the top of the business cycle. As you read the objectives listed below, decide which of them will work for you. Then make plans to implement them. The following are our Phase B Management Objectives™·

1. *Accelerate training.* Spend some of the increased income you take in during Phase B to train your workforce. The training you provide will pay for itself in the upcoming months and quarters because your personnel will be able to handle the increase in your business without missing a beat. Examine your operation and determine where you can improve your staff's efficiency and expertise because it will benefit both your company and your customers. Making your employees more valuable also makes your firm more valuable.

ALAN SAYS

When good people face challenges, they step up to the plate. Recently, I spoke with the CEO of a US manufacturing firm. His company was clearly in Phase B and loving every minute of it. Since the company was on a roll, he decided to upgrade equipment, a decision that required the company's machine operators to learn entirely new skill sets in order to run the new devices. I mentioned that the change (that dreaded word) might be hard for the machine operators to swallow because, after all, they had been working the same equipment for years.

I was wrong. The CEO told me that the machine operators embraced the change and the training that enabled them to grow with the times and to remain competitive. By the way, this company is solidly in Phase B while US Industrial Production is down 12.9% (3/12).

---

2. *Check your processes flow for potential bottlenecks.* Sure, you can handle the workload now, but what if the volume picks up another 5%, 10% or 20%? Could you handle the extra load? Do the analysis now, work through different scenarios to look for possible bottlenecks and determine how your systems will perform when new business pours in — as it will in Phase B. Making changes now will be a lot easier, and probably much cheaper, than fixing breakdowns that occur when your volume has increased.

3. *Continue to build inventory.* Building inventory in Phase B is important for two major reasons:

   a. The first reason is to avoid running out of stock, which will make your customers angry. They need their goods and don't want to wait. Delays may put them in a bind with their customers and if your competitors have what they need, your customer could say, "Adios" to you.

b. The second reason is to increase your margins. Since inflationary pressures often accompany Phase B, buy raw materials before their prices rise and keep more finished goods on hand. Building inventory will let you hold your prices while your competitors raise theirs — or you can raise your prices to match your competitors' increase and boost your profits. Either way you win! While building inventory may run against what the business gurus are presently advising, during Phase B, stocking up definitely makes sense.

BRIAN SAYS

A comment that we constantly hear during Phase B is, "I'm too busy." Although folks truly mean it, the comment always astounds me. If you're working too many long hours, stressing your resources to the limit and generally wondering what your family looks like because it's been so long since you saw them, get back to basics, Economics 101. You can adjust the demand for your products or services by *raising your prices*. Your supply curve can be the same or you can even scale it back, but your profits will go up…way up!

---

4. *Increase prices.* We touched on this above, but let's take it a step further. Let's assume you are busy, really busy. Your goods or services are in great demand and you're enjoying a nice return on your investment. As more business comes in, you notice that your people are feeling increased stress and your costs are going up because of mistakes, absences, increased inefficiencies, and overtime. Raise your prices. Now is the perfect time. At first, your level of activity may level off, but your profits will

increase, and you can deal with your cost problems in a sane, contemplative manner.

ECO-SENSE

Raising prices can be emotionally difficult. Many entrepreneurs consider the sales price of their goods or services to be an extension of or a reflection upon them. So when they raise their prices, they risk rejection, which nobody likes! If you have this feeling, remember these thoughts:

- You are not your product or service
- When someone says, "no," it is not personal
- When you are extremely busy, your goods or services are inherently worth more
- If you don't receive a fair price for your goods or services, you are doing your company a disservice

5. *Outsource.* Consider using outside manufacturing sources or subcontracting work when internal pressures start becoming tight. It's natural to want to expand internal capacity when the future looks bright and you identify long-term needs. The tendency is to add brick, mortar, and people thereby increasing your fixed costs and semi-fixed costs. Adding to your in-house capabilities, and therefore your costs, works best in these situations:

   a. You are entering a market in a new geographical area or offering a new product or service

   b. You have an extremely long building or buying time that requires you to look beyond business cycles

   c. You have a highly technical service or product to protect

BRIAN SAYS

Don't let success blind you to future opportunities. Most people are hard wired to think in straight lines. However, linear thinking in Phase B, particularly in the latter stages, can get you in all sorts of trouble. Instead of going by the book, looking straight ahead and thinking about spending capital or expanding your processes or the goods and services that got you this far, expand your vision and look in all directions.

Check what's lurking at the fringes, around the corner, above, below, to the side and in the distance. Ask yourself what new or related entrepreneurial endeavors you could develop to work for you.

6. *Open distribution centers.* A wide and short pipeline gives you great advantages. (A) It enables you to reach customers faster than your competitors and (B) lets you give them an increased service, expertise, and diversity on the same level that distributors provide.

MAKE YOUR MOVE>>> As you get busier in Phase B, so will your distributors. Work with them as you both take on additional loads by being more sensitive to their needs and the needs of your ultimate customers. Be flexible, willing to change and adapt because doing business as you did in the last business cycle probably won't cut it any longer.

7. *Use improved cash flow to improve corporate governance.* Develop a system to monitor and provide consistently seamless management. Review all your policies and processes. Then change and fix whatever isn't running smoothly. The changes you make will improve your efficiency and the bottom line now and in the long run.

8. *Use cash to create new competitive advantages.* We are firmly convinced that to prosper in the post-recession economy, every business must have clearly stated competitive advantages. The benefits of having such advantages have been fully detailed by our friend Jaynie L. Smyth (jsmith@smartadvantage.com) and William G. Flanagan in their brilliant book, *Creating Competitive Advantage* (Doubleday, 2006). We suggest you read it.

Smith and Flanagan's core premise is that very few companies fully understand the difference between a strength and competitive advantage. Smith's company, Smart Advantage, Inc., often uncovers scores of existing competitive advantages that businesses have not previously identified and used in their sales and marketing. Therefore, price often becomes the tie-breaker when their customers make buying decisions.

CEO-oriented organizations can be extremely beneficial. One of our favorites is Vistage International˚, otherwise known as TEC in Wisconsin and parts of Michigan. These organizations can give you an outside perspective on what is happening in business. They can also act as an objective, although unofficial, board of directors that will have only the health and welfare of you and your business in mind.

Creating Competitive Advantage cautions organizations to avoid "dangerous disparity" —the difference between what a company thinks customers value and the actual reasons behind customers' buying decisions. The key question is: Are you selling A, B and C, when the customer wants D, E and F? "Be careful that you are creating competitive advantages that customers value, not what you think they 'should' value," Smith warns. According to their research, which is based on customer feedback, the hierarchy of buying criteria often differs greatly from what sellers think.

MAKE YOUR MOVE>>> Align your competitive advantages with your customers needs. When you do, don't forget to clearly communicate your competitive advantages throughout your firm and your known universe. While you're in Phase B, spend money on advertising and promotions centered on your advantages. Take this opportunity to build a brand that will help maintain your margins and market position in the forthcoming Phase C.

9. *Watch your debt-to-equity ratio and return-on investment (ROI).* Don't lose sight of your financial guidelines and goals. The prospect of ongoing and seeming endless growth might tempt you to lower your standards or accept more risk than may be prudent. Remember the mortgage industry in 2007! Don't forget your goals and values and keep your financial compass pointed in the right direction.

    Watch your debt. The best time to take on the debt that will propel you into the future is early in Phase A when the rising trend is just forming and interest rates are low. Unfortunately, many people wait until they're late in Phase B and are absolutely certain that a rising trend is taking place before they seek to leverage opportunities. Cautiously take on debt for those items that will propel you into new markets to counter balance the cyclical pressures you may encounter. We have found that it really pays to finance missionary efforts into new markets.

10. *Maintain and pursue quality.* Quality counts and can give you a huge competitive advantage. Most companies don't want their quality to drop, but it nevertheless does with all-too-much frequency. While you're focused on pursuing growth, complacency can set in and lessen the quality of your products or services. Tie the constant need for top quality to Management Objective™ #6, using your cash flow to improve company governance and make it a top ongoing priority.

When it seems like the entire world is craving your goods or services, it can be hard to maintain your quality. However, if you let it drop, even the slightest amount, it can kill your reputation and all your years of hard, top notch work. Commit to continually providing the highest quality goods and services. It's what customers want and deserve. It's also a great long-term formula for beating the business cycle.

Holding it together

After you identify what it will take to keep your company profitable, turn your attention to what it will need for the long term. After Phase B, Phases C, D, and A are sure to follow. So plan and prepare for them. In your planning, take a broader perspective: Think in terms of orchestras rather than instruments; marathons instead of sprints; and decades instead of years. Then consider taking the following steps:

11. *Asking "What next?* Your answers to this question will help you identify how you want your business to develop, create an overall plan and identify the steps that will lead you to that destination. When you know what's next, you prolong your Phase B prosperity and make the next phase in the business cycle, Phase C, shorter. Your answers can also help you avoid painful Phase D.

    a. Figuring out what's next can be difficult. So start by reviewing your objectives, what you want. For example, we all want to continually grow our revenues, even in deteriorating or adverse economic conditions. Answer the following questions. They will help you decide what's next.

        i. What do I want to be 2 to 5 years from now? Do I want to be the non-executive CEO with an active company president who takes care of daily operations?

        ii. What do I want my company to be like in the future?

iii. Will my company develop a comprehensive market strategy? Will it be scalable?

iv. What new services and products will my customers require next year or a few years thereafter?

v. What will my customers need that they don't know about yet?

vi. Can I anticipate my customers' needs and fulfill them before my competitors are aware of those needs?

vii. Do export opportunities exist that I have yet to consider?

Companies that don't change are bound to fail. Look at your goals for your life, your wishes for your company. Assess your capabilities and your customers' real and perceived needs. Determine how you're going to meet each of them.

12. *Begin missionary efforts into new markets.* Look in new and different areas. Some direction can be obtained by determining "what's next." Identify new geographic markets (domestic or international) or new services or products that will create a new market that you can offer to your existing customers or to a new group of customers who are within your reach. Use your cash and governance to grow in *new directions*, not just to expand your present business.

13. *Manage your inventory.* As you near the top of Phase B, managing your inventory becomes increasingly crucial. Keep a large stock of your A items and begin to moderate your B items based on the impending slack in demand. Don't stock too many C items as you don't want to be left with slower movers when the economy and your markets slow.

MAKE YOUR MOVE>>> To accurately gauge future demand, apply the rate-of-change methodology to the sales of your specific product lines. Go a step further and track cyclical inventory changes using the same rate-of-change methodology.

Early in this decade, one of our clients, a senior VP at Parker Hannifin Corp., saved his firm $1 million when he reduced the carrying costs his company would have incurred. He used rates-of-change and the US Industrial Production forecasts that we published in EcoTrends® to determine when his clients' orders would begin to wane. In essence, he spent $795 and saved $1 million. Not bad!

14. *Penetrate selected new accounts.* Look for potential customers in counter-cyclical or in acyclical industries. As we've mentioned, acyclical industries include the medical, climate change, and green industries. We will cover them in greater detail in Chapter 11.

    While you're riding high in Phase B, offset the pressures that you will feel in Phase C by loading up on as many new customers as you can. Although this strategy may seem basic, you would be surprised how often it's overlooked by companies that focus on pursuing more business from their existing customers in Phase B.

15. *Plan for less activity in traditional, mature markets.* Determine how you will offset the slower growth that your company will face in the upcoming Phase C. What pricing strategies and long-term contracts will provide your company with a consistent cash flow? Phase B is an ideal time to fill your pipeline with as many orders as possible from your existing clients and from missionary efforts into new markets in anticipation of leaner days.

    Contractors provide a great example of how to take advantage of decreased activity. When the economy is strong, overhead and profit margins expand regardless of whether contractors bid or negotiate for work. Most contractors scale back when they notice a lot more competitors on bid lists *and* after they lose some contracts they would have ordinarily won. Usually, someone else filled their pipeline because they perceived a shift in future biddable projects.

MAKE YOUR MOVE>>> To spot these shifts before your competitors, use rate-of-change analysis. Then you can beat them early and often by shaving your overhead and profit margin. This strategy will enable you to remain both busy and profitable in leaner times while your competitors bid on subsequent projects in order to generate cash.

16. *Freeze you expansion plans.* Don't expand unless the expansion is related to your answer to Step 1 above, "What next." We can't over emphasize the importance of this Management Objective™. The optimism and euphoria of Phase B leads many decision makers to move into expansion mode when they approach the top of this business cycle phase. We've all seen it — firms that take on huge expansion projects only to sell them off a few years later when they need cash.

Follow the old axiom: Buy low (in the business cycle) and sell high! You don't want to expand at the top, when everything costs you more. So expand in Phase A or early Phase B, when your costs will be less.

ALAN SAYS

The early 1990s was a time of mild recession. We were hired by a firm that sold an upscale product that we forecast would be displaced by a competitor's less-expensive goods. We told our client to expect substantially decreased sales, but its management was optimistic, had a can-do attitude and a healthy dose of "not us." Management knew

---

that macroeconomic troubles would occur, but was convinced that the company would not be touched because "things were going so well!"

At the top of the business cycle, our client made substantial capital expenditures —just in time to see its sales plummet in Phase D. It wasn't long before most of the management team lost their jobs and the distressed company was purchased by a competitor.

17. *Spin off weak operations.* Look at your operation, evaluate all segments, and put the weak units up for sale. Spin off segments:

   a. That are only marginally profitable even in good times, or

   b. Have a long cyclical decline ahead of them.

Think in terms of the auto parts makers in 2007. They now wish that they had transitioned into manufacturing medical devices.

Don't be sentimental. Get rid of weak segments even though they may have been the core of the business or near and dear to the founders or senior management.

18. *Work for others.* Consider taking subcontracting work if the backside of the cycle looks recessionary so you can stay busy and keep your assets in place. Subcontract work may be less profitable, but it will give your company a profit center while the economy winds down.

Bud Mingledorff, Chairman of the Board of Mingledorff's Inc., an EcoTrends˚ subscriber, put it best. His company had one layoff in 35 years in business and that occurred during the Great Recession of 2008-09. Bud's philosophy is, "Laying off good people is like closing a store and leaving your inventory behind. You have a lot invested, so don't throw it away." Bud, we totally agree.

19. *Stay realistic.* Beware of straight line or linear budgets. They often cause gross misallocations of resources with resultant profit losses. When resources are misused, publically traded companies and their management take big hits from Wall Street.

Business leaders have the responsibility to be good stewards of their resources and making rate-of-change analysis can help. Linear budgeting is essentially straight-line thinking. It's not always helpful in unusual situations; it can thwart creativity and flexibility and can generate straight line forecasting. Throw in a healthy dose of the "not me" syndrome and you have a prescription for disaster.

Think about selling

Phase B is infused with a tremendous amount of enthusiasm and optimism regarding the future. It also creates a climate filled with new ideas, excitement and maximum goodwill. Even the most experienced, savvy buyers are buoyed by a few years of good news. The positive atmosphere, combined with your company's healthy profits, will push multiples up. So it can be a fabulous time to sell your business.

Emotionally separate yourself from your company (this can be extremely hard). Take several steps back and try to be objective. Selling your firm in late Phase B is selling at the peak, when profits, performance and prospects have hit new highs. Plus, you should get the best price. However, selling in Phase B also means getting out when you may feel least like it because everything is doing so well and looks so promising.

Study the forecasts for the next few years. If a steep, elongated recession is anticipated you may want to rethink work-out provisions, in which you are paid on the basis of a company's future earnings, or payments tied to the company's future profitability. On the other hand, a shrewd buy-back provision that gives you the right of first refusal to buy the company back if something goes awry could enable you to pocket some serious cash now and then, in a couple of years, get the company back at a much cheaper price.

George Livingston, Chairman of Realvest Partners, a Florida Real Estate brokerage, management and development company, sold two buildings at the top of the business cycle because ITR® raised warning flags about troublesome future trends. He based his decision on our forecast of an impending slump in the Florida real estate market and made the sale even though his partners urged him not to sell. His company realized high returns by selling the properties in the fourth quarter of 2007 and the first quarter of 2008. George's only regret is that he waited six weeks to sell the second property because the delay cost his company $180,000.

Cycles turn. George is now positioned to use the cash he received from the sales to buy low and obtain permits for new projects. He knows that the downward trend will turn into a new rising trend and is ready to capitalize on that change.

Be courageous

When you're at the top of Phase B, you may have to summon up a substantial dose of courage because some of our Management Objectives™ are counter-intuitive. Plus, everyone else may be blinded by your company's prosperity.

When your business is going great, you may be the lone voice calling for change. Your Board may be shouting, "Expand," while you're saying, "Spin off." When you ask, "What's next," your staff may protest, "We're doing enough!" At the top of Phase B, you may feel isolated and all alone because you want to hit the breaks when everyone else wants to accelerate.

Be courageous and stand your ground. Get others to see the light by using rates-of-change and leading indicators to buttress your positions.

Show them the figures and forecasts. Give them solid evidence, strong, reasoned arguments for the moves you advocate.

In June 2007, EcoTrends® advised its readers to get out of the stock market. The Dow was then at 14,000 and most people were bullish. Jim Perry, owner of OfficeScapes, in Denver, Colorado, took our advice even though the consensus was that the stock market would climb higher. Jim moved his 401(k) into an interest-bearing instrument that produced a 22% return while the average yield for the company's 401(k) was 6% to 7%.

In September that same year, Jim was looking to buy office furniture dealerships in Phoenix, but was concerned because he would have to borrow heavily. He consulted with Brian who was negative about the investment because our research showed that the economy in Phoenix had peaked. Jim decided not to buy, the economy in Phoenix tanked and Jim credits us for helping him avoid big losses.

Remember

Phase B is the best portion of the business cycle because it's a time of accelerating growth. Decisions made in early in Phase B will reap favorable returns. Although you may be running around and putting out "fires," business will be relatively easy compared to the recent recessionary years. Plus, Phase B is usually lots of fun.

Our Phase B Management Objectives™ are designed to propel your company higher and to keep it there longer than would otherwise be expected given prevailing economic winds. Carefully review these objectives and remember that they may be counterintuitive and uncomfortable to implement. However, the rewards can be huge and can position your company to beat the economy during the economic backslide that will inevitably come.

CHAPTER 9
MANAGEMENT OBJECTIVES™ FOR PHASE C

Every action must be due to one or other of seven causes: chance,
nature, compulsion, habit, reasoning, anger or appetite.

Aristotle

Once again, ABM Corp's management team has gathered for the company's quarterly review. You and the rest of the team are feeling good because the company is still growing even though the economy and your industry are moving below the levels of a year ago. As a result of your Phase B planning, the figures look like this:

Series	12/12 High	12/12 as of Jun 09
US Industrial Production	Jan. 08	- 7.6%
Our industry	Aug. 08	-10.2%
ABM Corp.	Feb. 09	3.7%

ABM's Phase B Management Objectives™ have been successful. Its 12/12 rate-of-change has increased over the last 11 months. That's longer than the longest-normal lag time for US Industrial Production, which is seven months. ABM has surpassed its industry through the peak by six months. ABM's 12/12 rate of change shows that it is still running above the level of one year ago by 3.7% while the economy and its industry have moved deeper into recession. It enjoyed six extra months of growth and expanded its profits, which has made everyone at ABM feel great!

However, signs for concern are appearing on the horizon as you can see from the figures below:

ABM Series	12/12 High	12/12 as of Jun 09
Core Operations	Sep. 08	- 7.7%
New Initiative	N/A	13.4%
Backlog	July 08	-12.1%

ABM's new initiatives have done their job: the company is 3.7% above year-ago levels on the strength of a 13.4% gain generated by the new initiatives the company implemented. Despite the good news, management is starting to realize that its core business is feeling the full fury of the recession. Since that core makes up the bulk of its business, ABM is now in Phase C. Although it has surpassed its levels one year ago, ABM's margins have slipped.

Since ABM is now in Phase C, it's time for action:

1. Make sure the company is ready for more Phase C and
2. Determine whether the company will be heading into Phase D after Phase C.

What is Phase C

Phase C occurs when the 12/12 rate-of-change has passed through a cyclical high and is descending toward the zero line. In Phase C, your volume of business (measured in either volume or dollars) is still higher than it was the previous year, but the increases are progressively declining. The 12/12 is on the backside of the business cycle and in the early portion of Phase C, the data trend's rate of ascent is slowing and will eventually move into decline before Phase C is over. See Chart 9-1 below.

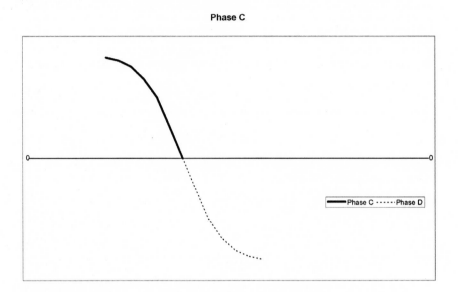

Chart 9-1: Phase C 12/12 is declining toward zero.

Early Phase C is a great time in the business cycle because your cash flow is strong and your optimism remains high. You are the captain of your ship and are sailing smoothly at a top speed. Everyone is delighted with how well things are going, including your customers, who are acting like they are still in Phase B.

Although it will take a while for the storm clouds to form in the distance, the leading indicators and rate-of-change tools have detected changes and warn you of the dangers that lie ahead. At this time, several reactions are typical and should be avoided. They include:

- The tendency to dismiss the early signs of impending economic problems as temporary matters that can be quickly and effectively controlled. Usually, the first signals of change are dismissed by outside authorities such as the Federal Reserve, central banks, and governments.

- The development of capacity constraints. Management may be looking to quickly bring new, expensive capacity online under the mistaken belief that the good times will continue indefinitely and customer demand will continue to grow.

- The desire to expand core operations and no longer be involved in acyclical or countercyclical markets. Since your company is making money and can barely meet the current demand, some of your people may not want to put resources into unproven areas.

ECO-SENSE

Bringing new capacity online in Phase C can be dangerous. It's often expensive because prices usually increase as the general economy becomes stronger and grows. If businesses expand just before the rising trend peaks and the downturn begins, they can incur higher fixed costs and underutilize expensive assets. For those reasons, we encourage you to expand when you hit your stride in early Phase B because it will help you keep the good times rolling and the profits streaming in.

Personal challenges

The early stages of Phase C can also pose challenges for leaders. A CEO who starts to make plans for lower levels of activity can expect some push back from the management team and even the Board. To defuse their resistance, keep everyone up to date on rate-of-change activity and explain why making Phase C plans are so necessary.

Human nature is also a factor. Allen Hauge, the senior Vistage Chair™ in St. Louis, Missouri, put it this way. "In Phase B, it's 'look what I did,' but in Phase C we shift to 'who is doing this to me.' As leaders, we must not look to blame others for what is happening. Instead, we need to communicate to everyone that this is not their fault and that they have not failed. The economy is too large a force for us to ignore or control."

On the success side of the ledger is Rick McCarten, the president of the Canadian Electrical Manufacturers Representatives Association, a Trade Association. Rick knew that during the impending economic downturn the association's member companies would have losses and those losses would decrease the revenues that the association took in. So Rick told his staff that (1) he was pleased with the outstanding work they were doing and (2) they were not responsible for the losses that the association would incur. Although both the member companies and the association did suffer losses, the association lost less than expected because of Rick kept his staff in the loop. By communicating with his employees, Rick kept their morale high so they did not resist the association's cost-saving measures, second-guess management or shift the blame.

Denial can be a difficult personal challenge in Phase C. It may be easier to wait and not act — especially since business is good and profits are high. When you're sleeping snuggly in the middle of the night, you may not want to find out what made that noise downstairs. So you might pull the covers over your head and try to go back to sleep.

Although denial is a part of human nature, leaders can't afford to ignore the signs. They must overcome their resistance by promptly taking *all* warnings seriously, examining them and determining what they mean. Then they must develop strategies and implement tactics to prevent potential problems from snowballing into disasters.

ALAN SAYS

In 2009, the automobile industry hit rock bottom. Retail auto sales fell 30.5% by the middle of the year. In the midst of this nightmare, Monique Ullom, President of CVM Autopark sent me the following letter. It's one of my favorites.

Hello Alan,

I don't know if you would remember me. I was in Rick Oppenheimer's Vistage® group in Lancaster. I was the one who didn't want to listen to you because I found your warnings too scary. But you convinced me to stay and listen twice. I want to thank you. I did listen to you and trend our business as you suggested and we have been able to weather the automotive crisis thus far.

When everyone else was singing about how great the economy was, I was preparing. Getting our departments stronger, keeping tight control on inventory levels, trimming the fat from our expenses since 2006 and saving for a rainy day has really paid off. I tell everyone who asks me how we are staying pretty healthy I tell them I listened to a great economist, Alan Beaulieu.

Will Phase D follow?

Phase C is short and shallow and the ABM's 12/12 rate-of-change has not dropped below zero. Although its rate of growth will slow, ABM's revenue stream will probably just flatten out before it resumes its rising trend. If so, management will not want to derail the Phase B initiatives that it put in place two to six quarters ago.

The question then becomes whether ABM should continue with its Phase B Management Objectives™ and move onto to its Phase C Management Objectives™. The answer to that question depends on finding out whether ABM will slide down the Phase C slope into Phase D or whether its move into Phase C is only temporary.

BRIAN SAYS

It's easy for management and the board of directors to downplay the risks of another downturn especially as they move further away from the last recession. They've learned to ignore the gloom and doom economists who mistakenly see the next recession lurking around every corner. If you examine your company's history via our rate-of-change methodology and plot it against the general macroeconomic business cycle, you will understand that today's good times and upbeat feelings are as normal as the slowdowns and recessions that will occur in the future.

If you pay attention, read the signs and prepare, Phase D can be avoided; it's not carved in granite.

To determine if Phase C will be short or the beginning of a longer slide into Phase D, ABM must:

1. Look at the leading indicators and determine the input for its 12/12 rate-of-change. As long as the input is declining, ABM can be sure that it will also feel the negative pressure caused by the business cycle. The timing relationships to the leading indicators should help ABM time out the trough. So if ABM checks its leading indicators, sees that they are all still going down and that the one with the longest lead time is 12 months, it will know that its downturn will be at least 12 months.

2. Examine its 3/12 rate-of-change. ABM has already determined the timing relationship between its 3/12 and its 12/12; therefore as long as its 3/12 is negative, it can be confident that its 12/12 will continue to move lower. The longer the 12/12 declines, the

more likely it is that it will move below the zero line and into Phase D.

3. Review the general economic forecasts, the industry forecasts and ABM's relationship to both. If a reliable source calls for the general economy to have less activity than a year ago in ABM's markets, ABM's activity will probably fall below the levels it reached a year ago — unless compelling reasons to the contrary exist. Examples of compelling reasons could be ABM's introduction of a revolutionary new product or one of its key competitors going out of business.

4. Finally, determining the length of Phase C and whether Phase D will follow is not a function of faith, but of reason. Make plans that utilize the Management Objectives™ presented below and implement them when both the internal and external factors point to (A) an ongoing decline and (B) the strong likelihood that the activity level will fall below zero.

BRIAN SAYS

Remember to think a half business cycle ahead. Decide what you will do when and if certain events occur. Use the leading indicators and rate-of-change tools to set up trigger or action points, times when you will turn your thoughts into actual plans and implement them. It's a three-step process: (1) think, (2) plan and (3) implement.

Thinking and planning based on the economic road signs will put you ahead of the curve and cost you nothing in terms of missed opportunities. Implementing plans based on the factual cyclical input will save you money, time and increase your profit opportunities.

Management Objectives™

Make the best of Phase C, by implementing the following steps. Read all of these Management Objectives™, select the ones that will work best for your business and then implement them.

The overall theme of the Phase C Management Objectives™ is caution. Be cautious and prepare your company for less business in your current core businesses, lower profits and erosion of your cash position. The following are Phase C Management Objectives™:

1. *Concentrate on cash and balance sheet.* The best way to proceed is to remember the old, but true maxim, *Cash is King*. Since the bottom line is the most frequent and obvious measure of a CEO's success, concentrate on it. However, prepare for slower growth and potential decline by giving your balance sheet a good hard look. As you do, ask yourself the following questions:

    a. Does your balance sheet depict a healthy company? If you check your balance sheet during the healthiest part of the business cycle and find room for improvement, you may have to do some heavy lifting when you think about the decline that lies ahead. You might have to pay off debt, beef up your cash position, and trim inventories.

    b. Do you have a depth of strength that you can draw upon in the coming quarters?

    c. Can you survive the next year if your business continues to soften and eventually starts to fall away? At what rate are you burning through cash, and can you support spending at this rate in the future?

    d. Will you be out of covenant on loan agreements? Make sure you can meet the terms of your loan agreements because in the next two years, you don't want to have liquidity problems because your lines of credit were withdrawn or called.

e. Will your debt to equity ratio prohibit you from borrowing more money in the leaner months that may lie ahead? Since you want your business to expand, see if using leverage could be the best way to go. Expand at the bottom of the business cycle, when prices, including interest rates, are relatively low. Even though your business goes through Phase C and/or Phase D, you should be able to expand if you're not cash poor.

f. Are your receivables and payables under control? Are they current and can you keep them that way? When cyclical conditions begin to deteriorate, many companies don't focus on keeping their receivables current. However, keeping receivables current must be ongoing in your company. Failure to manage your receivables can seriously harm your company as it heads into other phases of the business cycle.

When you answer these questions, prepare for stormy waters. Work with your accountant and finance team to come up with the best solutions. Who wants a leaky boat during a storm?

Bob Berk is a Vistage Chair™ in Chicago. He runs several groups; one is Vistage° group 307. After an ITR° presentation in 2007, Bob had his member companies start preparing for the current downturn in an ongoing and organized way. At every meeting, Bob prominently posted our action items. Although his members may have felt the downturn to varying degrees, Bob got them *all* ready for it. Amazingly, Bob didn't lose one member because of the downturn.

One of Bob's members is in the housing industry in South Chicago. While his business is down by 70%, this member is sanguine because he still has 18 months of cash saved up in the war chest he built because he believed us. Bob is rightfully proud of what he and his members have been able to accomplish in the face of daunting odds.

2. *Begin work force reductions.* Many firms are "slow to fire and quick to hire." However, in Phase C, they should be, "Quick to fire and slow to hire."

> In Phase C >>> Let them go
> In Phase A <<< Bring them back.

In early Phase C, let natural attrition help you reduce your staff. Then follow the steps below to accomplish your goals of conserving cash and preparing for lower activity levels. Although it can be hard to let employees go, it's often necessary for your company's greater good. Ultimately, it may also be better for good employees who are on the wrong bus.

As your company progresses further into Phase C and conditions continue to soften, take the following steps:

- Identify your A, B, and C personnel early in Phase C.

- Set metrics to use to determine when the time comes to let people go. For example, when your 12/12 rate-of-change sinks to a 1% growth rate, when Earnings Before Interest Depreciation and Amortization (EBIDA) reaches 3% or when you foresee that you will have significant cash issues in another four months if you remain on your present course.

- Make a list of the employees you will let go. Once you make this decision, much of the emotional pressures will subside and you will have time to mentally prepare for the actual reduction in force, which is always a difficult task. As businesses grow, it's normal for them to accumulate excess or less-than-stellar personnel and trimming that fat is a normal and necessary management function.

ALAN SAYS

Whenever possible, avoid multiple (layered) layoffs. They can increase employee uncertainty in your leadership and can be emotionally unsettling for your remaining employees. Both will erode productivity and profitability.

Also avoid across-the-board pay cuts. Good, hard-working employees often feel slighted. They feel that their contributions are not appreciated or properly rewarded because they received the same treatment as less or non-productive employees. Although across-the-board cuts may seem egalitarian, they erode loyalty and can impact employees' performance for years to come. They also give your competitors the opportunity to steal some of your top people, with all of their know how, simply by offering to pay them at their pre-cut levels.

3. *Set budget reduction goals by departments.* Coming up with realistic budgets based on slower growth and the possibility of eventual decline may seem simple, but it can be difficult. For the past few years, your company's mantra may have been "growth, always growth" and the philosophy "grow or die." However, since the economic downturn, the reality is that growth will level off and contract. So your expectations and resource allocations should be elastic enough to account for the changes that lie ahead.

Home Depot doesn't stock snow shovels in the summer because they're not in demand. Adjust your resources to cover not just a short seasonal period, but also a cyclical period that could encompass a multitude of quarters.

Keep in mind:

a. Production schedules for people and machinery, raw material orders and inventory levels for finished goods should be driven by the anticipated cyclical demand.

b. Projected cash flow for both inbound and outbound needs will also be impacted by changing business cycle conditions. This means your ability to satisfy your creditors will be at stake. It could also affect your ability to make payroll.

c. Projected profitability and your ability to meet targets will determine how Wall Street, your Board of Directors, business partners, or other stakeholders react. In effect, they, or some combination of them, will judge your management capabilities regarding how well you utilize the factors of productions and deliver profits in good or bad times.

d. Credibility with your customers, clients, staff, and suppliers will be dependent on the goals you set and how well you reach them. Make sure that you have metrics in place to determine when goals are achieved and who within your organization is accountable for meeting them.

4. *Reduce advertising.* Reduction in advertising levels is controversial in many quarters. Usually, the decision to reduce cash outflow for advertising will depend on your position vis-à-vis the market. In 2009, it would make no sense for a lumberyard to spend a fortune on advertising aimed at homebuilders. Conversely, it would make great sense for that lumberyard to spend money advertising to homeowners in order to convince them to buy energy-saving and do-it-yourself items. Identify your advertising targets and make sure to spend your money by tightly focusing on these targets.

Generally, business-to-business advertising is less effective on the backside of the business cycle. Focus more on business-to-consumer advertising.

5. *Cut training.* Selectively put parts of your personnel training on hold. Although it makes no sense to train employees who may be working for someone else in a few months, your senior accounting staff may need continual training to stay up with new and ever-changing tax laws, regulations, and interpretations.

   If you find that lack of employee preparedness and capability is putting you at a competitive disadvantage, you may have to step up their training. Consider *cross training* key people so they can wear multiple hats and perform multiple tasks. For example, after taking a class or two, a less expensive junior executive might be able to handle more responsibility or one of your warehouse workers could learn how to operate a forklift or your inventory control system.

MAKE YOUR MOVE>>> As you move toward Phase D, the demands on your work force will decrease in your core areas. So save training dollars now, but put those savings aside for Phase A, when the economy is advancing because in Phase A, your staff will have to be in command of the latest skills and technology.

6. *Deemphasize commodity priced products and services.* Anticipate diminishing margins. Commodity prices generally move lower, either in conjunction with or lagging behind, the decreased level of demand associated with the backside of the business cycle. Products are considered to be commodity priced when they are available from a number of sources and the consumer bases his or her buying decision primarily on price. If you operate an office cleaning service in conjunction with a more specialized restaurant sanitation service, the cleaning service might be

hard to distinguish from one company to the next. However, if the sanitation service is specialized and has higher standards of training, equipment, technology and results, its charges are unique, not commodity priced. So it can earn higher margins.

7. *Weed out inferior products.* Lose the losers. Eliminating inferior products requires you to take a closer look and implement more draconian measures than merely reducing or cutting back. Your beloved old Chevy, the one on which you and your siblings learned to drive, still runs — barely. But it smokes like a chimney, eats up gas and oil and isn't safe. You only dare to take it for very short rides. Although everyone has an emotional connection to it and doesn't want it to go, it takes up space, is rusting away, and serves no useful purpose.

MAKE YOUR MOVE>>> Most businesses have their old clunkers. Find yours and say goodbye. **WARNING**: — expect angst and loud emotional reactions, especially from those who have close, strong, sentimental attachments to what you want to cut. They can even get personal. Be tough and do what you have to do.

Phase C is the time to focus on the most profitable parts of your business. Stop wasting valuable resources on marginally profitable work. Concentrate on your most profitable areas and on fattening your cash cow.

8. *Avoid long-term purchase commitments late in Phase C.* Prices for commodities and many other goods tend to move in conjunction with, or lag slightly behind, the four phases of the business cycle. Prices usually drop when the general economy is in Phase C and especially when it is moving into Phase D.

Aluminum is a good example. The 12/12 rate-of-change for the price of aluminum moves consistently with the US Industrial

Production 12/12. Let's go back to June 2008 and see how it works.

a) In June 2008, most folks were wondering what the characteristics of the US recession would be.

b) Internally, your management team wondered how your company would fare in the downturn.

c) Based on credible forecasts, you know the recession will be steep and by using rate-of-change methodology, you know that your 12/12 will soon follow suit.

d) Purchasing wants to buy 200,000 pounds of aluminum at $3.090 per pound. The amount is more than you usually buy at one time, but prices, although vacillating, have been generally climbing since February 2007.

Do you buy or do you wait?

If you buy, you must spend $618,000 now. Most people think that if you wait, the price will rise even higher. So if you delay, it could cost you more. Your instinct is to buy a lot now and lock in prices.

You decide to wait because of the forecasts of a weakening general economic environment. Three months later, prices start to fall.

e) In September 2008, you buy 100,000 pounds at $2.461 per pound.

f) In December you buy another 50,000 pounds at $1.438. Since your sales and orders have dropped off, your inventory needs are less — so you buy less.

g) Your total cash outlay is $318,000. You saved $300,000 by paying attention to where you and the economy were in the business cycle and by having a reliable methodology that told you where you would be in the future. If you had bought the full 200,000 pounds of aluminum as originally planned, your saving would have been $228,100.

9. *Decrease inventory.* Lower your bloated inventory. The more inventory you have on hand, the more it costs you. So keep your stock at levels that are sufficient to meet your customers and clients' demands.

   If you're a distributor, you will have to anticipate your customers' needs and balance your lines in accordance with the declining inventory levels your customers will need. By decreasing your inventory, you will cut your carrying costs. The main questions you must answer are: Should you reduce all of your lines or just some? How should you decide which lines to cut?

MAKE YOUR MOVE>>> Use rate-of-change methodology for each product groupings or large lines to select where you need to stock less inventory. For example, Product A may be an item for the electricity-related market that is selling well, while Product B, which is for the automotive market, is not. Your inventory levels for Product B should be adjusted, but not those for Product A.

10. *Identify and overcome competitive disadvantages.* In our discussions of Phase A and Phase B, we dealt with the creation of competitive advantages. In Phase C, identify and fix any competitive *disadvantage* as you head further down the business cycle slope. Competitive disadvantages can cause you to lose customers for many reasons:

    a. Slow deliveries
    b. Poor or barely adequate quality

    c. Dated brands and messages. For example, don't encourage your customers "to put tiger in your tank." Instead, tell them to "move into the increased mileage world."

    d. Not using the latest and expected technology. As a survey company, are you using a laser transit with a handheld computer-recording device? Is your data processing as efficient or as up-to-date as your competitors? Are you the last gas station not accepting debit cards?

    e. Packaging that is viewed as environmentally unfriendly or wasteful.

11. *Make sure you and the management teams are not in denial.* If straight-line forecasting becomes a group event, which it easily can become, it can lead to all kinds of budgetary and resource allocation problems. Like most problems, the cure for these matters is best when applied in a preventative fashion. Keep your team aware of the internal and external rates-of-change, leading indicators and industry forecasts to build credibility and teamwork, and keep everyone in the loop and on the same page.

12. *Watch Accounts Receivables.* Pay close attention to aging receivables. Don't let your past due ratio grow faster than your sales. Phase C is an ideal time to listen to your accounting staff when they tell you to be careful with how much credit you extend and to whom you extend it.

Be prepared to deal with the competing interests of the good folks in the sales and accounting departments:

- Sales have a pedal-to-the-metal mindset and want to bring in orders through any and all means, including extending the most favorable credit terms.

- Accounting can see that many of today's sales will be tomorrow's collection problems when the economy deteriorates and eventually moves into Phase D.

You can't make everybody happy. However, remember this:

- If you *lose a sale* because the potential customer didn't have good enough credit, it will only cost you *the profit you would have made on that sale*.

- If you make the sale and subsequently have to write off the entire sale amount as uncollectible, it will cost you more. The amount you lose could be equal to the profit from many sales.

13. *Increase the requirements to justify capital expenditures.* In late Phase B and early Phase C, it's tempting to spend money on "more." During those phases, everything is going well and everyone is optimistic. When caution signs appear, denial may take hold because everyone is positive that they can keep it going forever if they just:

   a) Add more people
   b) Buy more equipment
   c) Upgrade their systems.

In early Phase C, many companies will add all sorts of items: a plant, another shift, a new line of automated equipment, a new fleet of trucks or a new computer system in the mistaken belief that this will keep the good times rolling. These expenditures can sow the seeds for future cash crunches that can force you into bankruptcy or unwanted mergers.

Instead, invest your capital to push into new markets. Also spend on items that will give you a quick payback and have the potential to bring in more cash. Examples include: extensions to your existing capabilities, green offshoots of your business, new, more efficient equipment, export markets and aftermarket service.

14. *Evaluate vendors for strength.* Make sure that your vendors are solid financially and operationally. Do your homework and find out if they can survive Phase C and Phase D. For each supplier ask:

    a) Does the management team understand what is going on in the economy and in the industry?

    b) Is it adding fixed costs and shelling out cash based on the mistaken assumption that the good times will last through the next two years?

    c) Keep an eye on your distributors. Their health is important to you and it's essential that they can supply what you need on time. Encourage them to think about cutting their inventories.

If your vendors are financially weak and in danger of failing, it could leave you with the expensive problem of covering the service and warranties those vendors would normally provide. When your suppliers can't deliver to you, you may not be able to deliver to your customers or clients. If your vendors go under, it could quickly put you at a serious competitive disadvantage and drain your cash.

MAKE YOUR MOVE>>> Check your vendors' condition, conduct research and ask hard questions. You will be glad you did.

15. *Manage backlog through pricing and delivery.* Fill the funnel. As you may recall, we advised you to start this process in the latter stages of Phase B. Now, step it up a few notches. Push to bring in more orders from new markets and existing customers or

clients because they will be optimistic from Phase B and their belief that prices will rise.

Get more aggressive:

a) Hold prices steady while your competitors increase theirs. This strategy will attract new customers and clients and will keep your existing customers happy that you are their provider. It can be particularly effective if you increased your prices earlier and established a reasonable profit margin.

b) Offer incentives for customers and clients to enter into long-term contracts with staggered delivery times.

c) Use the cost saving measures you have implemented to maintain your profit margins in a weakening pricing environment.

Cancellations will impact your backlog, but a well-thought-out cancellation policy and some give-and-take on your part will go a long way to enhance your customer relationships. You should end up with enough wind in your sails to push you through the coming doldrums, at least through a good part of it.

ALAN SAYS

Communicate with your management team and line personnel. If all they see is you piling on work and diminished margins, they might question your sanity. Keep them informed by laying out your plans and telling them what you are doing and what you hope to accomplish. Some of the points to touch on with your staff include:

1. Explaining what Phase C and Phase D are and how long you think each will last

2. Telling them that you appreciate the extra efforts they will have to make in the next few months

---

3. Stating that although you cannot add to your fixed cost structure at this time, if their efforts help build a backlog to go forward, they will be rewarded accordingly
4. Pointing out how the backlog will provide jobs in the coming recession
5. Noting that you expect your competitors to be unprepared and that many of those firms will be required to make layoffs as the economy deteriorates
6. Giving assurances that by working hard now, the company and they will be better off tomorrow and in years to come.

Remember

Phase C is about caution — in terms of decisions and the potential dangers that may lie ahead. In Phase C you're running full speed ahead, but then the road narrows and curves. So you have to slow down and apply the brakes. Had you checked out the road in advance, you would have known when to cut your speed, slide into the curves and not risk losing control.

In Phase C, plan conservatively for cut backs; focus on building up your cash and positioning your company for the future. It takes *progressive* planning and being adept enough to manage slowing activity in some business units while simultaneously lighting the entrepreneurial fires that attract business from new markets. Firms that successfully navigate Phase C maintain their profitability and successfully lay the groundwork for the opportunities that arise in late Phase D and early Phase A.

Once again, remember that some of our Management Objectives™ for Phase C may be counter-intuitive at the times they should be implemented. When that occurs, as it probably will, try to look toward the future instead of simply today. It will give you greater confidence in our approach, which will sharpen your radar while others just gaze at the stars.

THEO ETZEL, Conditioned Air, Naples, Florida

- ¬ Company was founded in 1956.
- ¬ Theo Etzel took over in 1995.

OVERALL: EcoTrends'® forecasts convinced Conditioned Air to move out of a market before it collapsed and focus on new business opportunities in areas where the company could be the dominant player and position itself for greater future growth.

METHODOLOGY:

Theo reads EcoTrends® for trends in commercial construction, and also focuses on housing starts, the Purchasing Managers' Index, the money supply and the Federal Reserve Board data. Theo reviews the economic indicators he receives through EcoTrends˙ at his monthly management meetings.

Background

- From the time Theo took control of Conditioned Air, the company rode the tract home boom in Southwest Florida.

- Conditioned Air expanded into custom residences where air conditioning systems can run from $100,000 to $1 million in large, luxury homes.

- When the Florida housing market was flying high, Theo was asked to expand his company's presence in the tract home market. Expansion would have boosted Conditioned Air's business from $8 million to $12 million.

- In the third quarter of 2005, when the market still seemed to be booming, Theo, based on ITR˙ forecasts, concluded that the trend would not continue. So he decided not to invest in added infrastructure, tools, trucks, and people and sought opportunities where Conditioned Air did not have a significant presence.

- Conditioned Air took the funds otherwise earmarked for infrastructure in its well-established lines of business and poured them into service, maintenance and the retro fit market. To improve its technology, the company increased the number of its service technicians from 15 to 32.

Ongoing

Conditioned Air passed on making a short-term potential $3 million gain, which turned out well because the Florida housing market soon started to crumble and then went "over the cliff." Fortunately, the company was prepared. Theo is convinced that redirecting its focus helped build a better company. He believes that it will give Conditioned Air long-lasting benefits far greater than the $3 million it would have made.

As we go to press, Theo continues to follow our EcoTrends˙ reports to spot new trends. Conditioned Air has been able to ride the ascent in the residential aftermarket and the commercial construction market. Theo's moves have enabled Conditioned Air to boost its brand and reputation and it now services nearly all of the 500-700 unit projects that are being built in the area.

"Diversification and rebalance of focus got us around that mine field," Theo explained.

Chapter 10
Management Objectives™ for Phase D

The more urgent the need for a decision, the less apparent becomes the identity of the decision-maker.

Murphy's Eighteenth Law

September 2013: How long has it been since you've seen all those furrowed brows, those worried looks on your colleagues' faces? Three or four years? However long it's been, it doesn't seem long enough! Now, unlike in other downturns, you and most of the leadership at ABM Corp. understand business cycles - the ups and downs - and steps you must take. You and your team can think ahead, forecast and plan for a brighter tomorrow.

Isn't it amazing how blind so many of your colleagues are? They refuse to follow the signals. Even though they see the leading indicators moving lower and watch their own 12/12 rates-of-change starting to dip below the 100 line, they still argue that their companies are not in recession. They think that they're immune and can just ride out this downturn.

Wait it out? Forget it, you have to act now!

Phase D of the business cycle is when your 12/12 rate-of-change is declining below the zero line and your 12MMT revenue (or whatever other data series you track) is moving lower. During Phase D, emotions run high. People have different feelings on different days and their responses will vary:

1. "This is only a temporary, short-term deviation".
2. "The economy is not a factor and *we* can stop this slide any time".
3. "Nothing has changed. We're not going through difficult times." They're in denial.
4. "It's the big one and we're done for now." The fair-weather, inexperienced managers have been listening to way too much news. Some of them are paralyzed while the others head for the lifeboats.
5. "OK, yes, the seas will be getting rough; so let's ready the ship, adjust our course and keep moving." These are our heroes — the ones who adjust to reality without losing their way or giving up on their dreams. They stay calm, acknowledge reality and adjust without abandoning their dreams.

How do you ready the ship, keep it sailing on course, and navigate out of danger? The answer is by following our Management Objectives™, which are explained below. First, there are 10 powerful steps to take right away and then, 3 more that are even stronger to use late in Phase D.

Phase D

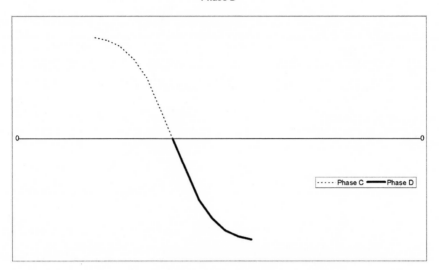

Chart 10-1: Phase D. 12/12 descending further and further below zero

10 Powerful Steps

Despite declining revenues, companies can remain profitable in Phase D. They can remain profitable and position themselves for the future by carrying out the following Management Objectives™:

1. *Continue work force reduction.* In Phase C, you identified your A, B, and C employees and discussed reducing the size of your payroll. Continue the process through attrition and by direct action on your part. Remember that the sooner your make the difficult decision as to whom to let go, the healthier your company will be and the more jobs you will ultimately save.

ECO-SENSE

As the leader, your primary job is to insure your company's long-term profitability. Tweaking the workforce, adjusting it to your company's needs and conditions and upgrading selected skill positions is part of the business cycle process — it's a part of your job. However, it may make you very unpopular.

2. *Reduce advertising – be very selective.* We understand the value of keeping your company's name in front of the buying public. However, we question the wisdom of expending money on advertising during difficult times in the light of the limited return on investment that it produces. For example, why should a company like DR Horton spend $15 million on advertising when its brand is strong and the housing market has virtually dried up? What purpose would its advertising serve?

On the other hand, it makes sense for an automobile dealership to advertise its superior service department and offer specials that will generate more revenue by bringing people into its showroom while their tires are being rotated. If advertising will drive revenues, it can be a wise move.

MAKE YOUR MOVE>>> If you decide to advertise, be extremely selective. Before you shell out your hard earned cash on advertising, ask yourself the following questions:

A. Is there a buying public that your advertising will influence?
B. Will your market position and brand recognition erode if you cut back on advertising during this downturn?
C. Do you have a compelling story that will be seen as a real help to potential customers in this Phase D environment?
D. Can you clearly enunciate your competitive advantages to those few consumers who may be buying?

3. *Avoid long-term purchasing commitments.* If you're used to locking in costs with long-term contracts, factor in that the prices for most goods and many services tend to follow the business cycle downward. So limit your inventory purchases when the economy is in Phase D. If you buy less, you can keep a handle on your costs and give yourself some wiggle room on your selling price. If you can give your customers price breaks,

it will be a real benefit to them that they will appreciate. And it won't negatively impact your bottom line.

Service prices may lag behind commodity prices in Phase D, but they usually follow suit. In response to the decline, firms may adopt more creative pricing strategies or offer more price bundling in order to bring in additional business.

Keep your commitments short because as you move to the bottom of Phase D, you will be able to get more favorable rates, which will save you money. Also review your agreements with your service providers to see if you can lock in low costs. If you can, it can provide savings that will directly impact your bottom line and six months from now, you may have more leverage and a better idea of what skills you will need as you move your company forward.

4. *Review all lease agreements.* In Phase D, vacancies are up; therefore landlords can have problems with their cash flow if their debt services, taxes, insurance, and maintenance costs are not elastic. These landlords want stable, paying tenants so you may be able to strike good deals and create win/win situations. Most landlords will listen to the following suggestions, all of which are designed to immediately improve your situation. Approach your landlord and with these suggestions:

   A. Lowering your monthly lease payment for the next 6 to 12 months by 20% and adding that sum to the last six months of your lease. Here's how it works. Let's assume you *save* $17,000 a month for six months for a total of $102,000. That direct savings will immediately flow directly to your bottom line. We don't need to tell you about the time-value advantages of saving money now and repaying it later with no accrued interest.

B. In addition, Phase A is coming and it usually brings some inflation. That means that the higher lease payments that you pay down the road will be made with cheaper dollars. So your savings will be equal to the rate of inflation plus the time value of the $102,000. Your landlord will win because you will still be a steadily paying tenant that helps its cash flow come at an acceptable pace.

C. Eliminating your lease payment for six months, but committing to an extension of the term of the lease for an agreed upon period, which may be a few years. In a severe recession, you may be able to successfully negotiate this type of cash saving plan. If you can, it will give you the advantage of having level lease payments later in what will probably be an inflationary environment.

D. Keeping your lease payment constant, but asking for upgrades in your current space or allowing you to move to upgraded space. A lease extension may be required. Many landlords will be happy to provide upgrades because it will continue their steady cash flow and keep a valuable tenant in place.

MAKE YOUR MOVE>>> Immediately send in your best negotiator. Don't wait! It doesn't matter that you may be early or in the middle of your lease term. Ask! Look for ways for both parties to win. Renegotiating leases can provide big savings for all sized companies. The only time this tactic will not work is when the owner of the tenant company is also the owner of the property.

5. *Increase your requirements for capital expenditures.* In the first half of Phase D, only a few good reasons exist to buy capital equipment.

A. The equipment will push your company into new markets that will offset the decline in your company's core activity.

B. The equipment has a long lead-time. It must be ordered now for it to be ready for Phase A.

C. The current cash savings are too good to pass up. Savings can be obtained from getting better terms, increased efficiencies, and new processes or decreased labor, to name just a few.

D. The equipment will provide you with a great technological advantage that will help drive prospects to you.

Near the bottom of Phase D, look at acquiring new and used capital equipment that can help you succeed in Phase A. Late in Phase D, the cost of capital equipment will be less than it was earlier in early Phase D. By waiting until late Phase D, your patience will be rewarded many times over by the profits you will make in the years to come.

BRIAN SAYS

One of the driving forces that motivate most entrepreneurs is the desire to hire hard working people who share their vision and will develop into dynamic teams that will ultimately enrich entire communities. Entrepreneurs like to be creative; they want to create products, services, businesses and jobs. They want to leave their mark and have broad, far-reaching success. However, they and other executives must keep in mind that the *long-term* interests of those communities are best served through the creation of profitable, honest, and fairly run companies that carry on, and even thrive, through the most difficult periods of the business cycle.

---

6. *Eliminate overtime.* During downturns, there is a natural tendency to want to help your people by providing them with the opportunity to earn overtime when the need arises. Giving employees overtime can be compassionate, commendable and, from time to time, clearly necessary. While adding overtime to fill large orders or serve new customers may be expedient, if it continues for extended periods, it can wreak havoc with your bottom line. Consider outsourcing work to qualified subcontractors or bringing in temporary contract labor to help fill your needs.

Solicit suggestions from your employees. Employees often have practical and insightful ideas on how to increase your efficiency and output and decrease costs. Their suggestions can help you maintain, and even improve, your productivity and profitability, which will help you protect future jobs.

7. *Reduce overhead labor.* Since your company will be having less activity, Phase D is an ideal time to trim your overhead labor force — those support people who are not involved in production or sales. Paying, supervising and managing fewer people will help keep your outlays down. Before making cuts, consider the following factors: tribal knowledge, people skills, future leadership potential and dedication. Make the tough decision even if it means saying goodbye to people you have known for years. Your main objective must be the greater good: benefiting your company and reshaping it to fit the current needs of the economy.

ALAN SAYS

As a rule, we are all rather slow to reduce labor, be it direct labor or overhead. We tend to put off difficult and unpleasant decisions. However, you have to bite the bullet and do what's best for your company and its future. As we previously stated, it helps to make your employment-priority list early and decide *in advance* at what point you will implement the decision.

8. *Combine departments with like capabilities and reduce management.* Look at your entire organization with an eye to streamlining its operations and organizational structure. In Phase B, you may have added capabilities, made room for specialties and compartmentalized operations, which turned out to be smart moves. However, times have changed and now that you're in Phase D, you may need to deconstruct what you carefully put together in Phase B.

   For instance, you operate an insurance agency that grew briskly from 2002 to 2008 along with the economy, and you made some changes. As the economy roared, you added staff to serve construction companies, to sell to the medical industry and to develop and sell financial planning products for young couples just starting out in life. You gave each group a support staff, a sales staff and a group supervisor, all of which were needed in the flurry of Phase B. Now in Phase D, you need to examine whether three separate support staffs and three supervisors still make sense — especially since the people who serve the construction industry are desperately trying to look busy whenever you walk by. Now, is the time to combine groups and protect your bottom line.

9. *Decrease selective prices to boost your business.* Cutting your prices may be wise especially if it will enable you to capture a great account, expand your product or service offerings, or get customers or clients to spend more money with you when the economy heats up again. This tactic works well if you adjust your cost structure so that you can offer price reductions that do

not decimate your profits. If you lower your prices, it will force your competitors who have not adjusted their cost structures to take profit-losing positions, which will hurt their cash flow and their ability to successfully rebound in Phase A.

Be careful how you lower prices because it can create problems when the recovery begins and you decide to raise them. When you cut your prices, make it clear to your clients and customers that the reductions are temporary. Call them "recession rollbacks" or state, "we are saving money on energy and want to pass the savings on to you."

ECO-SENSE

Service providers — As we've advised, it's best to lock your clients into long-term contracts at the top of the business cycle — late Phase B or early Phase C. If you have, great! If not, *now* is the time to become your clients' partner by offering to reduce each of your costs by suspending some of the secondary services you provide.

Find ways in which you can help your clients or customers. For example, offer to reduce a $60,000 computer maintenance contract to $50,000 provided you can decrease the services from five days a week to four. When you make your offer, emphasize that your client's financial health is important to you and that this reduction is being offered to help it weather this difficult time. Working with clients to lower their costs builds mutually beneficial relationships and generates good will. Showing you care about their welfare makes you a member of their team, a part of their family. When the recovery takes hold, you will be poised to resume full service and raise your prices.

10. *Tighten credit policies – increase scrutiny.* Take two important steps that your sales people probably won't appreciate. First, reformulate your credit policies to fit the times. Raise your

credit score requirements and those for Balance Sheet ratios before extending credit to new or existing (but marginally profitable) customers. Second, watch your receivables and don't be shy about trying to collect on time and cutting off credit when customers fall behind. Your accounting department is right; you can't afford to be lax when extending credit.

ALAN SAYS

Logically, it makes no sense to ease your credit requirements during a downturn. It is not your responsibility to finance your customers' operations and in a severe downturn, easing credit requirements can endanger your very existence. The following example illustrates this point.

Let's assume you want to sell a $400,000 boat to make a 20% profit. Mr. G.O. Away, a close-to-qualifying boat dealer, offers to buy your boat for the $400,000 asking price. The sales team is quite persuasive and the sale is made. 120 days later you are still trying to collect. 360 days later you write it off while the boat is sailing in foreign waters. $400,000 — gone. Had you said "no" to the dealer and passed on the sale, you would have lost $80,000 in potential profit. Now, you must sell five boats to make up that single write off ($80,000 x 5 = $400,000). *Vivre les accountants*!

Five months after entering Phase D

February 2015: ABM Corp. and the economy are in recession. ABM's revenues are falling and its bottom line has slipped. However, ABM has managed to stay profitable because it implemented our Phase D Management Objectives™ while most of its competitors are hemorrhaging cash and sinking further into the red.

The big question is "how much longer will the downturn last?" Three leading indicators have turned in positive directions and ABM has begun to fill in its Timing Analysis Table (see Chapter 5 to refresh your memory if you have not actually done a Table for yourself). At this time, the findings may be inconclusive, but they are encouraging because of the leading indicators' turn. It's beginning to look like a fourth-quarter-2015 low will be forming for ABM.

At this point, it's important for ABM to begin looking at our Phase A Management Objectives™ and for ABM's top brass to start talking regularly to its staff about the news that the leading indicators are forecasting. It is crucial to get everyone's mood and mindset turned toward recovery. It is also a good time to examine our last three Management Objectives™ because they are most powerful when the world is the most pessimistic.

Late Phase D Management Objectives™

1. *Grab distressed competitors' market share.* Firms that were caught off guard by the recession will have the greatest difficulty keeping pace. As Phase D drags on, they will find it especially difficult in the following areas:

   a. Innovation
   b. Introduction of new products
   c. Development and declaration of competitive advantages
   d. Marketing
   e. Advertising and promotions aimed at those that are still buying.

Turn your competitors' difficulties into opportunities. Move into their backyards and then trumpet your arrival. If your competitor sells the same hand-held power tool, tell the world about your new *energy-saving* hand-held tool that has longer battery life, can be recharged in less time, and is lighter, more durable, and fully guaranteed. Let your market see that your product or service is significantly better.

2. *Seize on opportunistic purchases of other companies.* The doom and gloom of the last few quarters still prevails. Interest rates remain low and peoples' expectations are even lower. Many firms have run out of cash, or will very soon. Others are depressed, discouraged and losing their will to fight as the recession drags on. As a result, many will be increasingly willing to sell their businesses or parts of them.

Now is the time to act. Start looking for firms in distress and begin conversations to purchase them or parts of them. Look to buy companies that would be good fits with your current operation and provide the most positive impact on your business in the next few years.

ONE OF OUR HEROES

Chris James of Womack Machine Supply Co., Farmers Branch, TX. CFO

As we go to press, Chris is getting ready to make his move. About 18 months ago, Chris had us do an Economic Timing Analysis for his company. Since then, Womack has kept it up to date and reviewed the results with its management team during its monthly staff meetings. Womack's 3/12 and 12/12 rates-of-change compare well with US Industrial Production and given its internal rate-of-change trends and our forecast for the US economy, the company has implemented strategies and is planning moves that will enable it to grow stronger in the coming Phase A.

According to Chris, as soon as the US Industrial Production 12/12 swings up, Womack Supply will make strategic acquisitions to take advantage of the change in direction of the general economy. Womack will be able to make these moves because it has been accumulating cash and expects to have sufficient funds on hand to implement its strategy. Given his past successes, you know that Chris will succeed with this late Phase D Management Objective™.

3. *Think about buying commercial property.* By the time you're in late Phase D, you will have a good handle on when the macroeconomic recovery will begin. As it now stands, commercial property construction and property prices are still lagging behind US Industrial Production. In addition, interest rates are always lowest during late Phase D of the business cycle and most people won't recognize that a recovery has begun until we are at lease one quarter into the recovery. You will have a great opportunity because during late Phase D, commercial property prices *will be* lower than they have been in years, interest rates will be favorable and the economy will be improving.

MAKE YOUR MOVE>>> Look for the right opportunities, conduct your due diligence and be patient. Keep in mind that you have one objective — to buy!

Use your newly acquired property to house your company's operations or lease the space to tenants to obtain cash to meet your debt service and carrying costs on the property.

WARNING: Be cautious with regard to your lease expectations and your anticipated cash flow. The prices for commercial property traditionally lag behind the economy; therefore the demand to lease your space could be a year or more away.

Bob Reinhart of Controls Link, Inc. has successfully acquired commercial properties. He sent Alan the following email:

Alan,

Thanks for your help in the past. If I don't see you at CSIA it is because I am closing on some great bargain properties. I really appreciate your newsletter and your help.

We were tired of low interest in passbook savings, and I'm not much of a stock kind of guy, so we decided to buy some bargain properties. Now, we have a 2000 square foot live/work property under contract in Tampa FL. It is in Ybor, which is a social center of Tampa and other engineering firms have offices there. It is one of the few places in Florida where you can walk to lunch and is also an enterprise zone and gives us a local presence where we see much work coming up (both in Tampa, Florida for water/ wastewater work). But in that sort of work, they want you to have a local presence. Not work right now, but stuff you can market to for a few years out. We're paying cash 130K, they were asking 149K. It is brand new as no one ever lived or used this property and they were asking over 400K two years ago.

Way to go Bob! In 10 to 20 years from now, many folks will be kicking themselves because they didn't follow in your footsteps and go bargain property hunting.

ECO-SENSE

Everyone won't be in Phase D at the same time. In fact, everyone may not experience Phase D. Your business may be in Phase B and fall no lower than Phase C in the next few years. If your business is in Phase B and the marketplace is in Phase D, remember that the marketplace will determine how you should act.

Use our three powerful Late Phase D Management Objectives™, adjust them to your situation and find the bargains that will appear during this special window of time. Capitalize on the abounding pessimism by taking over your competitors' market shares or by purchasing wobbly companies. Move into a new market and look vertically or horizontally for opportunities. Scoop up great deals on commercial property for straight investment purposes or to use for your own operation.

Nine months after entering Phase D

Be open to the probabilities of a developing recovery. Through analysis of your own rates-of-change, have the foresight to see that the initial signs of improving business for the company are consistent with what the leading indicators have been telling you should be happening. When these two factors are in synch, don't be afraid to start spending some money in anticipation of the upturn.

> *June 2015*: ABM Corp. has had a challenging three quarters, but is almost at the trough. It's time for it to get ready to move into Phase A. ABM's 3/12 is rising and it seems likely that it will soon move up past the 12/12, which will give it a second positive checking point. ABM's leading indicators are also rising and its timing analysis tells the company to expect a low in October 2015. Action calls. ABM has four months to do the following:
>
> - Complete its planning sessions and finalize its plans
> - Prepare its team for action
> - Get ready to spend some cash!
>
> When ABM takes these steps, it will be 6 to 12 months ahead of its competition. ABM will be reaping profits while its rivals are gasping for air.

Remember

In the early stages of Phase D, emotions, opinions and news will range from denial to despair. Many of your team members will be riding the same psychological rollercoaster. Help them stay focused by filling them in on the internal and external indicators that confirm that you have entered Phase D and signal when Phase D will end.

The bulk of the Phase D Management Objectives™ can be summed up as cut, conserve and consolidate. Jobs, positions and programs may be eliminated and your personal popularity may suffer. Take it in stride and remember that you are working to preserve and improve your company for the long haul.

In the late stages of Phase D, become more visionary and develop a sound strategy to accomplish your vision. Expect many of those around you to have difficulty understanding how you can be so forward looking "at a time like this." When you sense this reaction, know that you have added "leader" to your list of accomplishments.

CHAPTER 11
OPPORTUNITIES FOR TODAY AND TOMORROW

There is a tide in the affairs of men, which,
taken at the flood, leads on to fortune.

Shakespeare

In years gone by, blacksmiths played an essential role in industry and in an area's growth. Now, those once vital tradesmen are largely a thing of the past. So is an exhausting list of products such as horse buggies, hand-crank calculators, 8-Track players, lead-based house paint and dot matrix printers — to name just a few. And when these products disappeared, so did the service people who worked with them.

Technological and societal changes continually impact business. As they do, entire industries vanish. The economist Joseph Schumpeter called this process Creative Destruction and observed that it is a positive force for economic development over the long haul. Each item that we listed above has now been replaced by technologically superior goods that require more people, capital and management to make it succeed.

In light of the constant changes, continually ask yourself the following questions:

- What are the growth engines of tomorrow?
- What new businesses opportunities can we look forward to?

In this chapter, we will focus on seven areas that will provide exciting opportunities over the next decade, plus. Activity in these areas will not be as vulnerable to changes in the business cycle. The markets for these areas are at the forefront of long-term demographic trends and prevailing global political movements.

1. *Water*

Americans consider water pollution and fresh water shortages critical environmental issues. A survey conducted by GlobeScan, in cooperation with Circle of Blue, found that 88% of those surveyed worry that fresh-water shortages will become an increasingly severe problem worldwide.

According to the US General Accounting Office, at least 36 states reported that they anticipate water shortages in the next five years even though we currently have 100% access to safe drinking water in our cities and 94% in rural areas. Our daily domestic use is 570 liters a day per capita.

When it comes to future water needs, the US is not the only nation that deserves our attention. See if you know the answers to these questions.

- o What other country uses water so inefficiently in the production of goods that it consumes almost four times the world average?

- o What nation has a population of 1.2 billion people — three times that of the United States?

You guessed it, it's China. Since China is so inefficient, many of its people are forced to drink unhealthy, contaminated water.

Let's examine the following scenario and see what opportunities it presents. So much wastewater flows into China's rivers that three quarters of the rivers in China's urban areas are unfit for drinking or fishing. Amazingly, nearly a third of China's river water cannot be used for either industry or agriculture.

Chinese cities are suffering because of this pollution. Almost 90% of the aquifers are contaminated, which means that over 400 cities — out of a total of approximately 660 cities — have less water than they need and about 100 are grappling with severe shortages, according to the Council of Foreign Relations.

Water is just one of China's environmental issues. Other major problems include air pollution, soil erosion, deforestation and desertification. These dilemmas can all be fixed, but the costs will be enormous and cannot be resolved overnight. China's massive environmental troubles are one of the main reasons why we believe that China will not become an economic superpower in the next decade.

Think greywater. Europe and Australia define greywater as any water, except toilet water, that has been used in the home and then allowed to be used for landscape irrigation. The US also excludes kitchen sink water and water used to wash diapers (does anyone still do that?).

ECO-SENSE

Using greywater for landscaping meets the textbook definition of recycling because plants benefit from the small bits of compost not filtered out. Why irrigate with drinking water that people need when plants are better off with "used" water? We believe that the use of greywater and processes that will use greywater will only continue to grow.

OK, using greywater is legal and is certainly beneficial in that it reduces the amount of fresh water homeowners need. Since about half of all residential water is used outdoors, wouldn't you like to be the company that develops the system to reclaim household greywater for outdoor use? The size of the market for such a system will only grow over time.

It's reasonable to question whether greywater is safe and the answer is a resounding yes! In the US, greywater is used by an estimated 22 million people, businesses and governmental units. In the last 60 years, not one case of a greywater-transmitted illness has been documented. Although the smell may not always be pleasant, the profit potential clearly is.

MAKE YOUR MOVE>>> Concern about the safety and supply of water is global as are the opportunities for entrepreneurially minded companies. Working to reclaim water, increasing the efficiency of its use and making safe water available to industry, agriculture and hundreds of millions of human beings will provide businesses with growth opportunities that will extend far into the decades to come.

2. *Food*

Population growth and the increasing standard of living means that opportunities exist in producing, processing, shipping, distributing and selling food to the 6.6 billion people now alive and the millions more not yet born. Entrepreneurs will also find ripe opportunities in potential niche markets including ethnic and regional cuisine, as well as the health and organic food movements.

BRIAN SAYS

When you're thinking about the future, remember that demographics and economics make excellent companions. Adding more people to a capitalist-based business equation is one of the surest ways to grow your profits. Look for opportunities where the population is increasing and some semblance of an open-market system is in place. Keeping these factors in mind, some of my favorites outside the US are India, Indonesia, Brazil and Australia.

Where will food-related opportunities occur? Look for sustainable economic development because when a country's economy improves, its food supply normally follows suit. Find opportunities in producing, processing, distributing and marketing foodstuff of all kinds. The World Health Organization noted that populations all over the globe are eating different foods. They are moving from their traditional dietary staples, such as rice, roots and tubers, to more complex and Westernized diets that feature livestock products and vegetable oils.

The term "US Food Production" is defined for NAFTA compliance as industries that transform livestock and agricultural products into products for intermediate or final consumption. This includes retail bakeries and candy makers. Only twice since World War II has food production declined for more than four months: in 1974-75 and 2009. Over the last 20 years, the industry's growth rate has averaged 1.7%.

If you're thinking about entering the food industry, expect a steady, but not a rapid, rate of growth. US population estimates suggest that the growth rate in food production will stay healthy during the next 20 years as the population climbs over 400 million from the present 320 million.

Food-related opportunities have also been bolstered by a cultural trend: the marked propensity of more Americans to eat out. Although the restaurant business is notoriously competitive and the work demanding, the potential client base is huge and will support restaurateurs that have a clearly defined competitive advantage. Since January 1988, restaurant retail sales have annually grown an average of 5.6%, which is 2.4% above the average annual inflation rate for the same period. In food industries, real growth potential exists given our culture and population growth.

Keeping the food supply safe will also be a growth industry in the US and abroad. As industrialization and participation in the global market place rises, higher standards of living will occur worldwide. As they do, safety and health standards will also improve across the board. Health-related equipment, inspection and cleaning services will be in greater demand in the years to come.

3. Pets

It is amazing how many different creatures people have as their pets: dogs, cats, horses, fish, hamsters, turtles, rabbits, tarantulas, snakes, lizards and exotic birds. The list is enormous. We love our pets and are willing to sacrifice to take care of them. Although an increased number of pets end up in shelters during significant economic downturns, overall, the industry is recession proof.

Veterinarians earned an average of $89,450 as of May 2008, according to the Bureau of Labor Statistics, more than double the $42,270 figure for all occupations. The amount of out-of-pocket spending on veterinary services skyrocketed from $4.7 billion in 1989 to $24.1 billion in 2009. For the last 20 years, the annual growth rate of spending on veterinary services has ranged from 2.7% in 2009, which was a bad recession year, to 15.3% in 1995. The average annual growth rate over the last 20 years was 6.8%, which is well above the rate of inflation for that same time period. Expect more upside opportunities in the US and globally in the next decade.

Steady activity in veterinary practices bodes well for suppliers of medicines, medical equipment and other durable goods to the pet industry. Pet care, foods and supplies are also growth industries.

4. *Energy*

Increased industrialization and a commensurate increase in the standard of living globally tells us that the world will be consuming more energy in years to come. Technological breakthroughs will provide business opportunities in areas ranging from coal to renewable goods. And don't forget that oil and natural gas are not going away anytime soon.

Opportunities will abound in exploration, research, production, development, transmission, consumption efficiency and in addressing overriding environmental concerns. Although the risks of political and culturally related disruptions are large, the demand should drive up the supply and prices for many years.

Conservation efforts and the growth and long-term potential of the green movement will provide golden business opportunities. For example, consider LEED* (Leadership in Energy and Environmental Design) construction. Barron's, the weekly financial publication, predicts that existing commercial buildings that fail to upgrade to LEED* standards and new construction not built to LEED* norms, will become obsolete because their operating costs will be higher than LEED* buildings. LEED* structures also create healthier workplaces, boost productivity, and reduced absenteeism.

The list of potential users of LEED* construction methods, materials and practices includes more than just government and large businesses. It includes universities, hospitals and other medical facilities, non-profits and retail environments - all of which will be encouraged to think increasingly green in coming years. Private industry will be convinced by tax incentives, enhanced bottom lines and the facts that LEED* buildings lease faster and retain tenants better. When their profits increase, private companies will receive higher appraisals and greater access to financing.

<hr>

ALAN SAYS

Since the world of energy generation, distribution and consumption is so diverse, business leaders will have a myriad of ways to try to improve the standard of living for the world's inhabitants. Energy, despite its many forms, is a relative constant in economics. In the short term, its prices may fluctuate, but supply and demand tends to change at a glacial pace.

Energy generation and consumption patterns in one part of the globe aren't necessarily those that will be adopted in other areas. So when you look for your niche, be open to the various forms of energy and unique situations that vary from place to place.

Energy producers, manufacturers, distributors and end-user providers should benefit from the green movement for many years. As environmental awareness spreads and the demand for green buildings grows, LEED˚ certified contractors, and other green builders, will have a great competitive advantage. That advantage will enable them to increase their profits and the value they provide.

<hr>

5. *Healthcare*

In the coming years, medical and technological breakthroughs will extend people's lives and as the population ages, the healthcare marketplace will expand. By the year 2020, older patients may constitute up to 40% of the US population. They will be a large voting block and a huge consuming block. Each year, more people will need medical care and the *amount* of care they will need will increase. Businesses that serve the health needs of senior citizens will experience a peak of activity between 2020 and 2025.

Position your business to support healthcare providers or become a provider. Great opportunities will emerge because a virtually limitless range of goods and services will be needed to deal with all the ailments that attack the human body. To take advantage of those opportunities, learn about the healthcare industry, identify the directions in which it is moving and find niches that your company can fill.

Healthcare has become fertile ground in the search for new technologies - conquering the affects of aging, for example. Billions of dollars are annually invested in medical R&D and in the coming years, the search will continue and grow. It will spawn developments that we now can't imagine.

As the population grows so will the demand for more end-of-life services. There will be a greater call for estate planning: wills, trusts and advance medical directives such as living wills, do-not-resuscitate orders and powers of attorneys. People will also need more extended care services, quality of life services and funeral services for themselves, their families and even their pets.

6. *Lawyers and tax advisors*

In the next few years, we believe that a landslide of regulatory and tax changes will be aimed at business and "well-to-do" individuals. Since these changes will probably come at a fast and furious pace and at a significant cost, explaining them, interpreting them and deciding how they should be addressed will be a growth business.

MAKE YOUR MOVE>>> Businesses throughout the world must focus on protecting themselves from the growing movement that seeks to redistribute wealth. This movement wants to hit businesses with more and higher taxes in order to protect the public from the alleged greediness and irresponsibility of business, a position we categorically reject.

a) Make sure that you work with a top-notch tax specialist.

b) Pay your taxes when they are due and do not defer paying them until sometime in the future because we expect tax rates to increase.

c) Become involved in the legislative and regulatory process.

ECO-SENSE

Check www.fairtax.org, the website for Americans For Fair Taxation. This organization advocates the enactment of the FairTax Act, a nonpartisan proposal that would replace all federal income, gift and payroll-based taxes with a federal retail sales tax. This change would simplify the life of individuals and businesses, be a boon to our economy and a gift to our posterity. Currently, the FairTax has no realistic chance of becoming law, but the more Americans who become aware of it and vocally support it, the greater the likelihood that this landmark change could subsequently be adopted.

7. Security

The fiscal 2009 federal budget will probably allocate approximately $663 billion for defense spending and $42.7 billion for homeland security. We expect demands for security to increase in the near future. Many firms will find opportunities serve the defense and homeland security efforts. In the next few years, the defense budget will most likely be pared, but a great deal of money will still be available for businesses of all sizes. The bidding for government procurement contracts will be extremely competitive, but the list of products and services that the government will still need is going to be enormous.

Other types of security services will also be in demand. We believe that corporate security for multi-national firms, cyber security and personal security will also be growth industries in the years ahead.

Personal security will be of greater concern. In the past, it was enough to know your banker and lock your front door. However, technological advancements of the last several decades have increased the opportunities for evil to befall us without our learning about it until it is too late. Now we live in a world of hackers, identity thieves and cyber-con artists, Ponzi schemers and a wide assortment of crooks. Kids are vulnerable as soon as they leave home. The Internet has exposed us to an insidious new breed of criminals who can strike from anywhere - from the other side of the planet or your own backyard.

People are tired of being victimized. They're growing weary of electronic and identity theft and threats to their personal safety. So we believe that they will gobble up effective counter-measures as soon as they are developed.

As our cities and urban centers grow, people will demand more protection. They will want safer neighborhoods, schools and homes. More people will want to learn how to physically protect themselves. Since people aged 65 and older will be stronger, healthier and lead more active lives, they will want safe, secure places to live.

Remember

The seven items discussed in this chapter are not an all inclusive list. They are just the tip of the iceberg, and in the near future, many other exciting opportunities will appear. We chose each of the seven items covered to give you a taste of the possibilities that businesses will have and get you thinking about areas in which your company could move.

Go back, reread the seven items and think about them. After you read each one, list (1) the opportunities that it could present for you and your business now and in the future, and (2) list areas that you can explore and learn more about.

While each of these areas will provide great opportunities, please keep the basic business cycle in mind. In your analysis, use rate-of-change methodology for each target industry and company to identify where it is in the business cycle. Then use the leading indicators to look for opportunities outside your selected marketplace. By tracking general business cycle trends, you can determine when to expand, invest in upgrading your systems or adjusting your personnel.

TOP 10 FORECASTING RULES

1. Identify the most important data series to be analyzed.

2. Prioritize them. You can analyze the others later.

3. Go to our website www.ecotrends.org and get the template for creating your own rates-of-change.

4. Compute your company's rate-of-change.

5. Determine which of the four business cycle phases your company is in and how long it is likely to be in that phase.

6. Compare your company's rate-of-change with the trends in the overall economy and your industry.

7. Identify which leading indicators you will use to forecast your company's future.

8. Run a Timing Analysis using our Timing Analysis Table (see www.ecotrends.org).

9. Review our Management Objectives™ and determine which are appropriate for your company at this juncture.

10. Meet with your team, explain your objectives, lay out your action plan and the process you will take. Get their input.

Chapter 12
The Next Great Depression

The empires of the future are the empires of the mind.
                                    ---Winston Churchill

It's September 2030 and we are at our annual planning meeting. The economy is getting soft; we recognize that it's in Phase C. The warning signs tell us we will soon be moving into recession, into Phase D. So we make contingency plans accordingly and tell ourselves that enough economic controls are in place for a major contraction to be avoided.

Fast forward to September 2031. We are amazed at how quickly the economy tanked and that we are only one year into what now looks to be a multi-year event. The Great Depression scenario that had everyone scared to death in 2008-2009 seems to be here now. Sales are already off 50%, share prices are down 70% year-over-year and governments don't have the room to maneuver that they once had because of deficits and inflation.

The period ahead will be every bit as devastating as prior Great Depressions. Had we known that it was going to be *this bad*, we could have done things differently.

The coming storm

A high probability exists that the decade spanning 2030-2040 will be one of lost opportunities, great economic distress, lost fortunes, deep regrets and despair over what might have been. Protect yourself: Plan for this future and strive to stop it from occurring.

In this book, we have tried to show you that business cycles regularly occur and how to successfully manage during each business cycle phase. In order for your business to stay healthy and thrive, you must capitalize on the good times and understand how to prosper through the bad times because each of them will come.

In most cases, short-term economic imbalances lead to business cycle phases that last for three to four years. That's the usual case. However, these imbalances can also cause problems that may haunt us for a decade or longer.

Our dire predictions for 2030-2040 are based on four factors.

- Economic theory
- Deficits and Inflation
- Taxes
- Demographics

Note that each of these four contributing factors is beyond any single individual's control. If each of us changed our behavior, it would not stop this impending economic disaster. The driving forces are institutional and a depression is inevitable because of the inherent nature of man, of governments, and the self-interests of both.

At this time, we will not be providing in-depth analysis regarding the 2030-2040 period that lies in store. We will be writing another book that will deal exclusively and in detail with that lost decade. It will cover how to prepare for the next Great Depression, protect our families and what signposts will tell us if the trends for the four factors cited above are changing sufficiently to avert the severity of the downturn that we are forecasting.

Economic theory

Economic literature contains evidence of longer-term cyclical changes and theories on these longer-wave cycles. Instead of going into all that literature, we will rely on the theories, experience and results we have gained at the Institute for Trend Research, which forms the theoretical basis for our projection. These are the same factors that enabled ITR˚ to forecast that the early 1980s would be very difficult recession years and that the recession in 2008-2009 would be longer and more severe than any downturn we had recently seen.

History shows that capitalism is a winning methodology, especially when positive demographics exist. Despite our dire projections for 2030-2040, that impending depression will not necessarily spell the end of American economic dominance or the American way of life. However, we anticipate a severe and prolonged cyclical event that will last longer than a typical business cycle. The probability of such a severe downturn demands that you change your thinking and actions. The depression ahead will be rough but that doesn't mean that we are at the end of the era of American hegemony.

Let's think in general terms about what it would take to alter the future we foresee. First, let's agree that the future will be the outcome of trends that are now in place and will probably be in place in the coming years. If we can change those trends, then we can change the future.

Although change begins with a single individual, it must spread beyond that one person in order to have a great impact. It must become institutionalized. Many people, multitudes, must sign on. In trying to change the future, getting a sufficient mass is the most daunting challenge and three possible sources can lessen or derail our fears about 2030-2040.

- Leadership
- Selflessness
- Technology

<u>BRIAN SAYS</u>

Some combination of strong leadership, a change in attitudes and technological developments could render our outlook for 2030-2040 less severe. However, at this time, we think it unlikely that we will avoid the severity of the downturn ahead. On the optimistic side, a leader, a national consciousness or a technology might emerge that will alter the course of events. Unfortunately, we see no signs of any of them yet and history gives us little reason to believe that current trends will sufficiently change. But then, it could simply be different this time.

Deficits and inflation

Some folks will argue that long-term deficit spending, particularly by the government, is not harmful to the average person's economic well being. Others don't believe that inflation will negatively affect the economy. In the short term, they may be right, but over time, debt and inflation will take their toll.

Deficits (especially when you think about the mounting national debt) combined with the pernicious effects of inflation create an economic imbalance that puts more and more pressure on the economy. This pressure will make growth and prosperity unsustainable. If broad-based prosperity is to become a long-term reality and we are to avoid a depression, one or both of the factors (deficit spending or inflation) must sharply decrease.

The logic is straight forward. Deficits create increasing national debt. That debt carries a service charge (interest) that must be paid. Taking on debt when interest rates are cheap (as they have been through most of 2009) makes a great deal of sense as long as you are borrowing money to invest in wealth-creating assets. However, even borrowing to create wealth works best in the short-term, not when it's ongoing and decades-long.

In this look at deficits and inflation, we are not going to debate the "wealth creation" aspect of government spending as it applies to the public good. Instead, we want to emphasize that deficit financing is not an advisable one-time or even short-term economic strategy. The government's own projections through 2019 indicate that the annual federal deficit will range between $500 billion and $1 trillion.

- At the low end of this range (unlikely as it may be because of erroneously favorable growth assumptions), the US national debt will grow by 50% over the next 10 years alone.

- At the higher end of the scale, the size of our national debt will double in 10 years.

Unless a significant policy shift occurs in the US, we seem bound to add more and more to the national debt well beyond 2019.

The problem is not so much that we will owe money, but that we will have to pay more interest on the debt, particularly at a time of prolonged inflation such as we are projecting.

- Inflation means higher interest rates.

- Higher interest rates mean a larger part of the federal budget must be directed toward paying the interest on the increasing mound of debt.

We expect a significant crowding-out effect from increased spending. It also could mean that the government will have to increase its revenues to keep funding current programs. If you factor in the probability of new deals for special interest groups, you can see that the trend is untenable.

The Congressional Budget Office (CBO) estimates that 13.0% of the federal fiscal 2009 budget will go toward the government's debt service. Assuming only a very modest annual half percent point rise in the interest rate that the government must pay to attract needed capital (based on the CBO's own growth expectations which we think are overly upbeat), the 13% estimate for fiscal 2009 will grow to 25.5% in 2012 and 34.1% in 2015.

Think about the dilemmas politicians will face when they have less and less discretionary revenue to spend because more government funds are needed to pay for past decisions. Will they cut expenditures elsewhere to make up the difference? Or will they lean toward raising taxes to make up the short fall?

ECO-SENSE

The bind the government faces is really no different than what has happened to many individuals. They bought a home, a car and lots of consumer goods on credit. They made their monthly payments and their debt seemed manageable. However, when interest rates moved up, it became harder for them to make their payments.

These are the plain facts: spending must be cut in order for the government to meet yesterday's obligations; hard decisions must be made and life will get a lot tougher.

Taxes

If you were a wage earner from the early 1980s through 2008, you probably realized that your federal income marginal tax rate fell. Business leaders devised strategies around this unusual phenomenon and took it into consideration when planning for the future. Before long, the dual pressures of deficits and inflation will change the environment that most of us have known throughout our careers. As we move into the future, taxes will have to rise.

The perceived need for more and more government services that was spawned by the 2008-2009 downturn is the strongest the US has seen in modern times. After increasing steadily through the 1980s, the size of the federal government shrank significantly in the 1990s. A trend toward larger government began in 2000 and that trend has seen a dramatic spike in the past year. The pain of 2008-2009 convinced many that more government action is the answer.

It will become increasingly clear that the government needs more money from its citizens. Plan on higher taxes and on having less money to spend because the government will need to raise funds to pay the interest on its mounting debt.

In 2030-2040, the economy's resiliency will be weakened. We won't be able to count on consumers to make the necessary choices to correct cyclical imbalances because so much of their money will be consumed by taxes and so much wealth will be eroded by inflation. Instead, we will be increasingly dependent on government to make the right decisions at the right time.

It isn't the taxes per se that pose the most serious potential problem, it is the near certainty that the government will not be as efficient as consumers in allocating resources that would maximize economic growth.

ALAN SAYS

When I speak to groups, I try to make sure every audience understand that we are apolitical at ITR˚. Our view of what lies in store is not based on politics, personalities or political beliefs. The issues we see are not republican or democratic issues; they are spending and taxation issues. I am absolutely certain that both parties make huge mistakes and that both are capable of doing the right thing.

Demographics

The US population is aging; however, our population is still growing while those in many other countries such as Japan, Canada and some European nations are not. While population growth tends to create economic growth, the bulge in the number of older people between now and 2030 will pose challenges.

A growing demographic base that is ready, willing, and able to contribute to the economy would serve to mitigate the problems we project for 2030-2040. However, it will not be our older citizens because they will produce less and need more government furnished services. Today's toddlers won't be able to answer the call because it will take too much time for them to innovate, consume and pay taxes.

However, another group will help – immigrants. An influx of learned, hardworking and tax paying families could willingly contribute to and help support our way of life.

Underfunded programs for an aging and more needy society will create significant financial threats to our economy. These programs include Medicare, Medicaid and Social Security. In the years ahead, an additional strain will be caused by expenses for health care reform, military actions, the development of alternative forms of energy, safeguarding food and water and other programs. Their costs will be significantly compounded by the deficit, inflation and taxing issues already discussed.

The antidote to depression

Leadership: With the right leadership, a fundamental shift in a cultural trend toward selflessness and perhaps through technology, the magnitude of the forecasted decline in 2030-2040 could be averted. Please note that the probability of a recession occurring at that time will not go away completely because our business cycle theories have not changed. The extant factors to which we are looking are potential reasons for the severity of the cyclical decline that would be happening in the 2030–2040 decade.

In terms of leadership, it will take someone of enormous stature and charisma to shift us from our tendency to base our decision on "what's in it for me." We will need to adopt the concept espoused by President John F. Kennedy who encouraged us to ask what we can do *for our country*. We must also ask ourselves what can we do for the next generation — even if it means self-sacrifice today.

BRIAN SAYS

Many people think that we won't be able to find a leader who can put us on the right course. I believe that it will take more than one person; it will take a Congress of them. Can they do it? I hope so. I am hoping for mounting internal and external pressure to change the political reality and force Congress to respond. If we can't hope for change, we can only believe in a linear destiny. The future is our decision; whether we take advantage of the opportunities in front of us is another question.

To insure economic wellbeing and put our nation on the right course, we all need to pitch in. To meet the challenges of tomorrow, we must alter our attitudes and actions.

Selflessness must become a central part of our cultural identity. If we are unwilling to curtail our current consumption so that we can fund entitlement programs or change the present entitlement programs so the next generation can afford them, we will not be likely to escape a great depression in 2030-2040. Baby boomers will face the greatest burden and the greatest challenge. Hopefully, they will rise to meet this challenge. With age, wisdom is said to come. Let us hope it's true.

Technology. For many, technology is the great hope, the belief that future breakthroughs will help us avert possible future calamities. Wouldn't it be wonderful to envision a future in which our nation is the world's innovative incubator and the dominant economic force? We could become a source of technology that continually gives birth to new industries that become fountains of jobs, income and tax revenues. It could happen, but don't count on it because ultimately people (our natures, desires and appetites) drive economic trends.

MAKE YOUR MOVE>>>The trends we see are massive and have so much momentum that they will be difficult to change. Action is imperative. We need to implement economic moves that will protect us, to fight the good fight in an attempt to preclude the next Great Depression from hitting with unprecedented force.

We live in an amazing, resilient economy populated by incredibly bright and earnest people. However, a confluence of factors such as deficits, inflation, taxes, and demographics seem to be creating a near perfect economic storm on the horizon. The fact that these trends are already visible to some experts doesn't mean that the Great Depression of 2030-2040 won't happen.

ECO-SENSE

Should you retire in 2029? During normal business cycle recessions, we have advised some people to get out of the game and onto the sidelines. The Great Depression of 2030-2040 will be much deeper and worse than normal. So sell the business, retire, and get on the sidelines by 2029.

Remember

We frequently say, "The future is our decision" because all of us - individuals and businesses - can take advantage of future trends and make the future our own. What may be difficult to accomplish at an individual or business level can be nearly impossible at the macroeconomic level. The Great Depression of 2030-2040 isn't a certainty, but the probability is great. All the factors, the mass and momentum are in place and nothing to the contrary seems to be looming on the horizon.

Still, it's incumbent on us to try to alter the trends leading to a decade-long depression. Hope alone is not enough, action is critically necessary. Prepare your businesses and your finances and develop the means to protect your families and communities from what promises to be the next Great Depression.

The first step is to understand that the forces that will shape that downturn are now being unleashed and time is not on our side. We face a difficult task that we will address in detail in a later book. We must undertake that task not for our sake, but for our children's and our children's children - such is the size and scope of the 2030-2040 depression.

Chapter 13
Summing Up

It is only when we forget all our learning that we begin to know.
Henry David Thoreau

As we go to press, the US economy is showing signs of recovery. According to our forecasts, the economy will move into a widely recognized recovery in early 2010 but the rate of rise will be very mild. Many people will still be looking for jobs in the latter half of 2010. Inflation and higher interest rates, along with higher taxes, are anticipated for 2011 and beyond, but at least the level of economic activity will be noticeably improved both in the US and around the world.

No doubt about it, we've gone through a difficult period that will take years to reverse. While there is a recovery ahead, we do not see real growth to new record levels of activity returning to the US economy until sometime after 2013. Many corporations that were global giants no longer exist. Others needed bailout money to keep them afloat. Main Street is filled with vacancy signs and millions of Americans are still out of work. Many lost their homes and have had their lives turned upside down.

These changes sent everyone scurrying for answers and in search of culprits to blame. They castigated capitalism, business, government, our leaders, each other, and our way of life. They accused business of being greedy, exploitative, and corrupt. Doomsayers proclaimed the American era over; they declared that our economic and political dominance has come to pass. They compared our situation to the decline of the Roman Empire and warned that China would take our place.

They're wrong, dead wrong! The overall US economy is strong and our industrial base continues to grow long term. The US is the most productive nation in the world and will continue to be. According to the latest UN data, the US and Canada account for 23.6% of the world's total manufacturing, with the vast majority being produced in the US. By contrast, China accounts for only 13.7%.

Americans are inventive, hardworking, and productive. We constitute only 4.8% of the world's population, but generate 23.1% of the world's GDP. Based on those figures, we can do anything we set our mind to, including reversing the present downturn and continuing our role as the leader of the economic world.

Your work

Despite all the blaming, finger pointing and accusations, the business community here and abroad can hold its head high. The work you perform is essential and the effort you make is honorable — in fact, it's noble. You should be proud of what you do and the benefits you provide. Your work and the businesses you run don't just benefit you and your company; they help your employees, the nation and the world. Without your contribution, the world would be much worse off and looking for others to blame.

So don't listen to the doubters, the naysayers, and prophets of doom. Our economy is healthy in spite of this recent slump. It has gone through a severe recession, an inevitable phase of the business cycle; and although that recession was deep, our economy will rise again, be stronger and more powerful. In the future, our economic engine will roar into high gear and present you with many lucrative opportunities. Problems lay ahead such as 2030-2040, but they can be overcome as long as we live up to our heritage of innovation and self sacrifice.

So keep working, and working smart. Focus on the future. Follow the leading indicators to track the business cycle, identify where your business is in the cycle, and plan ahead. Use our Management Objectives™ to take the greatest advantage of each business cycle phase. Make your move into new areas that are less vulnerable to economic trends. Make your move to aggressively pursue opportunities at each phase of the cycle. You have the tools to make this happen.

The only limitation to your future is how much imagination and energy you bring to bear on determining your own fate.

Our thanks

Thank you for reading this book. We believe deeply in this country, our economic system, and you. Your hard work has made capitalism the best way to improve the standard of living for billions of people across this planet, and it has made this country great and will continue to keep it on top.

Please feel free to send us your questions and comments, and tell us how we can be of help.

About the Authors

One of the country's most informed economists, Alan Beaulieu is a principal of the Institute for Trend Research where he serves as President. Since 1990, he has been consulting with companies who have a domestic and global perspective on how to forecast, plan, and increase their profits based on business cycle trend analysis. Alan is also the Senior Economic Advisor to the NAW and the Chief Economist for HARDI.

Alan specializes in applied research regarding business-cycle trend analysis, growth-cycle trend analysis, and the utilization of cyclical analysis at a practical business level. He is a featured speaker at corporate and trade association meetings both in the U.S. and overseas and makes about 150 personal appearances each year. He has spoken to thousands of business leaders in manufacturing, healthcare, distribution, real estate, construction, and technology forums.

Prior to joining ITR˚, Alan operated and was a partner in several firms, where he developed great practical expertise. From the early 1980s to the early 1990s, he was also an adjunct faculty member at Daniel Webster College in Nashua, NH, a position he loved and that prepared him to get business leaders to understand and apply business cycle economics.

Pronouncements from the Institute for Trend Research and/or Mr. Beaulieu have appeared in/on: the *Wall Street Journal*, *New York Times*, *USA Today*, Knight Ridder News Services, Business Week, Associated Press, *The Washington Times*, CBS Radio, CNN Radio, Sirius talk radio, KABC, NPR affiliate WLRN and numerous other outlets.

Brian Beaulieu has been an economist with ITR* since 1982 and its CEO since 1987. He is also Chief Economist for Vistage International and TEC, global organizations comprised of over 13,000 CEO's. At ITR, Brian has been engaged in applied research regarding business cycle trend analysis and the utilization of that research at a practical business level. The thrust of the work is to provide companies with the means to anticipate economic changes before they happen in order to maximize growth and profit potential. For the past 26 years, he has been giving workshops and seminars across the US and Canada to thousands of business owners and executives in a wide range of industries. Prior to joining the Institute, Brian was an economist in Washington, DC for the US Department of Labor where he worked on the health care component of the Consumer Price Index.

Mr. Beaulieu's views have appeared in/on: *the Wall Street Journal, New York Times, Barron's, USA Today, CNBC TV, FOX Business TV, Knight Ridder News Services, Reuters, CBS Radio, the Washington Times, Atlanta Journal Constitution, KERA TV, Canadian TV,* and numerous other outlets. He is a regular columnist and contributing economist to national trade associations and publications.

The Institute for Trend Research

The Institute today makes approximately 275 presentations a year in a myriad of venues, reaching over 10,000 senior executives. Its clients include:

Target
Goodwill Industries
Michelin
Husqvarna NA

Honeywell International

Cushman & Wakefield

BAE Industries

Mitsubishi Electric

Stanley

Parker Hannifin

National Association of Wholesalers

Robert W. Baird

Graybar Electric

Van Andel Institute

Kennametal

Rockwell Automation

BUY A SHARE OF THE FUTURE IN YOUR COMMUNITY

These certificates make great holiday, graduation and birthday gifts that can be personalized with the recipient's name. The cost of one S.H.A.R.E. or one square foot is $54.17. The personalized certificate is suitable for framing and will state the number of shares purchased and the amount of each share, as well as the recipient's name. The home that you participate in "building" will last for many years and will continue to grow in value.

Here is a sample SHARE certificate:

YES, I WOULD LIKE TO HELP!

I support the work that Habitat for Humanity does and I want to be part of the excitement! As a donor, I will receive periodic updates on your construction activities but, more importantly, I know my gift will help a family in our community realize the dream of homeownership. I would like to SHARE in your efforts against substandard housing in my community! (Please print below)

PLEASE SEND ME _____ SHARES at $54.17 EACH = $ $_____

In Honor Of: _____

Occasion: (Circle One)   HOLIDAY   BIRTHDAY   ANNIVERSARY

      OTHER: _____

Address of Recipient: _____

Gift From: _____ *Donor Address:* _____

Donor Email: _____

I AM ENCLOSING A CHECK FOR $ $_____ PAYABLE TO HABITAT FOR HUMANITY <u>OR</u> PLEASE CHARGE MY VISA OR MASTERCARD *(CIRCLE ONE)*

Card Number _____ Expiration Date: _____

Name as it appears on Credit Card _____ Charge Amount $ _____

Signature _____

Billing Address _____

Telephone # Day _____ Eve _____

PLEASE NOTE: Your contribution is tax-deductible to the fullest extent allowed by law.
Habitat for Humanity • P.O. Box 1443 • Newport News, VA 23601 • 757-596-5553
www.HelpHabitatforHumanity.org

LaVergne, TN USA
08 December 2009
166335LV00004BA/2/P